What a fabulous job Karin D (with Kari Tumminia) have done book. They have managed to exp invaluable combination of EFT experience and useful stories from many clinical experts as well as draw from relevant neuroscience research. This text is an invaluable and well-documented resource that is a must for anyone using EFT tapping with clients or patients.

—Craig Weiner, DC, www.chirozone.net

This book is serious work, designed to give you insight, philosophy, and the attitude required to be successful in your practice. This is a training resource that will raise your EFT IQ to a new level, and additionally educate you on your business, website, and marketing. I know my ability to handle the sometimes turbulent waters of session work has been greatly enhanced by the authors' gift of genuine EFT wisdom. I have no doubt that I am by far wiser, and better prepared in my EFT practice having read this book.

—Ken Breen, Skillstotransform.com

Congratulations to Ann Adams and Karin Davidson on their latest EFT manual. Not merely a review of the information in the previous books, the EFT Level 3 Comprehensive Training Resource *is an authoritative, well-documented, and comprehensive review with references to scientific studies as well as real-life case study illustrations and insights. This is an invaluable resource for practitioners who are already well versed in EFT and are practicing or wish to practice at the clinical level.*

—Nancy Gnecco, MEd, LPC, EFT Founding Master, www.NancyGnecco.com

As I've come to expect from this superlative series, EFT Comprehensive Training Resources, *the new Level 3 edition delivers the same accessible, incisive commentary and steady lens through which to see the foundational underpinnings of EFT and related fields of psychology and quantum energy. Student and expert alike can find something to consider and something practical to take away immediately, expanding both horizon and capability.*

In the past, "Level 3" simply meant harnessing the power of EFT through our own "art of delivery." Now it enters a new era, one of mastery meeting meaning, expertly reflecting a mature EFT worldview for both the serious

energy practitioner and traditional licensed healthcare professionals alike. It's EFT for grown-ups—written to and for those who've come of age in their EFT practice and skill sets. I believe we've hit a new standard in EFT training resources, and I'm proud to recommend and use this rich volume with my students and mentees.

—Jondi Whitis, AAMET International Master Trainer of Trainers

This is a very well documented work on taking EFT to a higher level. With many quotes from the EFT world to illustrate concepts and many study cases, the authors have produced a tremendous compilation to guide our way into the practice of excellence.

—Eneas Guerriero, AAMET EFT Master Trainer, Germany and Brazil

EFT Level 3 Comprehensive Training Resource

Ann Adams and Karin Davidson,
with Kari Tumminia

www.EnergyPsychologyPress.com

Energy Psychology Press
3340 Fulton Rd., #442, Fulton, CA 95439
www.EnergyPsychologyPress.com

ISBN 978-1-60415-098-8

Cover design by Victoria Valentine
Editing by Stephanie Marohn
Illustrations by Kari Reed www.ArtbyKariReed.com
Typesetting by Karin Kinsey
Printed in USA
First Edition

10 9 8 7 6 5 4 3 2 1

Disclaimer

Please read the following before proceeding:

The information presented in this coursebook entitled *EFT Level 3 Comprehensive Training Resource* (the "coursebook"), including ideas, suggestions, techniques, and other materials, is educational in nature and is provided only as general information. The information presented in the coursebook is not intended to create and does not constitute any professional relationship between the reader and the authors and should not be relied upon as medical, psychological, coaching, or other professional advice of any kind or nature whatsoever.

This coursebook contains information regarding an innovative meridian-based healing technique called Emotional Freedom Techniques (EFT). EFT uses the ancient Chinese meridian system with a gentle tapping procedure that stimulates designated meridian end points on the face and body. Although EFT appears to have promising mental, spiritual, and physical benefits, it has yet to be fully researched by the Western academic, medical, and psychological communities and, therefore, is considered experimental. EFT is self-regulated and is considered "alternative" or "complementary" to the healing arts that are licensed in the United States.

Due to the experimental nature of EFT, that it is a relatively new healing approach, and because the extent of EFT's effectiveness, risks, and benefits are not fully known, you agree to assume and accept full responsibility for any and all risks associated with reading this coursebook and using EFT. You understand that if you choose to use EFT, it is possible that emotional or physical sensations or additional unresolved memories may surface, which could be perceived as negative side effects. Emotional material may continue to surface after using EFT, indicating that other issues may need to be addressed. Previously vivid or traumatic memories may fade, which could adversely impact your ability to provide detailed legal testimony regarding a traumatic incident.

EFT is not a substitute for medical or psychological treatment. You agree to consult with your professional health care provider for any specific medical problem or psychological disorder. In addition, you understand that any information contained in this coursebook is not to be considered a recommendation that you stop seeing any of your health care professionals or taking any prescribed medication, without consulting your health care professional, even if, after reading this coursebook and using EFT, it appears and indicates that such medication or therapy is unnecessary. The authors strongly advise that you seek professional advice as appropriate before using EFT, before implementing any protocol or opinion expressed in this coursebook, and before making any health decision.

If you intend to use EFT with others, you agree to use EFT only within your prescribed scope of practice, under appropriate ethical guidelines, and to comply with all applicable laws and regulations. Any stories or testimonials contained herein do not constitute a warranty, guarantee, or prediction regarding the outcome of an individual using EFT for any particular issue. Further, you understand the authors make no warranty, guarantee, or prediction regarding any outcome from you using EFT for any particular issue. While all materials and links to other resources are posted in good faith, the accuracy, validity, effectiveness, completeness, or usefulness of any information herein, as with any publication, cannot be guaranteed. The authors accept no responsibility or liability whatsoever for the use or misuse of the information provided here, including the use of information in links to other resources.

By continuing to read this coursebook, you agree to fully release, indemnify, and hold harmless, the authors, their respective heirs, personal representatives, agents, consultants, employees, and assigns from any claim or liability whatsoever and for any damage or injury, personal, financial, emotional, psychological, or otherwise that you may incur, arising at any time out of, or in relation to, your use of the information presented in this coursebook. If any court of law rules that any part of the Disclaimer is invalid, the Disclaimer stands as if those parts were struck out.

By continuing to read this coursebook, you agree to all of the above disclaimer.

Note: Though actual client cases have been used in this coursebook, names and other identifying information have been changed.

Contents

Introduction

Best-selling author, speaker, and entrepreneur Brian Tracy wrote, "Those people who develop the ability to continuously acquire new and better forms of knowledge that they apply to their work and lives will be the movers and shakers in our society for the indefinite future" (www.BrianTracy.com). Both Socrates and Yeats likened learning to the lighting of a flame that must be tended rather than to the finite filling of a pail. Albert Einstein suggested that learning should "commence at birth and cease only at death." As an EFT practitioner, whether you are beginning your Level 3 journey or revisiting information to refresh your skill set, there is nothing more important to your success in energy medicine or any other endeavor than your continual search for improvement and for new and better forms of knowledge.

This Level 3 training resource book was designed to introduce advanced EFT concepts, as well as review some previous material that the authors have found to be particularly important. EFT and other energy-based modalities are constantly evolving as we continue to understand more about how and why these noninvasive techniques work. The pathway to becoming an effective practitioner lies in your ongoing ability to expand your knowledge, add to your skill set, and refine the things you already know and use. Doing so will not only help you improve as a practitioner, but will also ensure that you are offering your actual and potential clients the best services possible. The goal of this Level 3 training resource is to aid you on your journey to continued learning, to introduce more advanced techniques for working with others using EFT, and to present Level 3 EFT concepts in the context of a greater academic understanding.

What to Do When EFT Seems Not to Be Working

One of the beautiful things about EFT, and often one of the things people are most drawn to initially, is the speed at which it can work. There are countless testimonials, anecdotes, and videos of people experiencing what many like to call "one-minute wonders." These examples of EFT resolving major issues in a single session are amazing to watch, so they are remembered and referred to often, but they represent the exception to the rule.

A more accurate representation of EFT and how it works is in the hard work and multiple sessions usually required for individuals to find complete resolution on a particular issue. Similarly, there are times when issues are especially stubborn, and it might appear that EFT is not working. These times are expected in any practice, and when they occur, there are several things practitioners can do to ensure that they are approaching stubborn issues as effectively as possible.

Specifics vs. Generalities

When working with EFT, one of the most common mistakes, and one that can make issues appear to be difficult or stubborn when they may not be, is applying EFT to a global or general issue. Specificity is one of the keystones of effective use of EFT. Ann Adams uses the catchy phrase "For results that are terrific, you have to be specific" to remind her students that while you might start out with a global issue or general tapping, it is not until you have gotten to the specific—time or place or person—that the most effective, deep work with long-range results is completed. This concept of getting to a time, place, and person is shared by existing therapeutic modalities. For instance, psychiatrist David Burns, MD, a specialist in cognitive behavioral therapy, states, "You can never help your client until the problem is defined around a specific person, place, and time" (Mitchell, 2009, p. 19).

Although EFT works best on a specific event, it can be as simple as starting your session with, "When I woke up this morning, I stayed in bed with the covers over my head because I felt so depressed. As I think about this morning, I am still feeling hopelessness as a heavy weight on my shoulders." Granted that you, as a practitioner, will explore further to discover what's behind this, including other times and places these feelings were prevalent, but this example gives a starting place for tapping. You have a time, place, and person.

Aspects

Addressing the various aspects of what is seemingly a single issue is also paramount to EFT's success. Missing any of the many potential individual aspects of each presenting issue is another mistake that can make it seem that EFT "isn't working." As you have already learned, EFT works best when it is applied to very specific events, memories, or feelings. Generally speaking, most issues are far more complex than they appear at first presentation or first explanation. They typically require multiple sessions with numerous conditioned response pairings (Feinstein, Eden, & Craig, 2005). The complexities of issues are based in the multiple components, angles, and causes of what might initially appear to be a singular issue. It is in the process of grappling with these complexities that a thorough understanding of aspects is necessary (Davidson & Sherrod, 2013, pp. 209–218).

In the Level 1 manual, we used the illustration of a puzzle to help you understand core issues and aspects. In this example, if you were to think of an issue as a puzzle, aspects are the individual pieces that make up the larger image. You might have also heard the idea of aspects described as an onion in which individual issues could have many layers that need to be peeled away to allow resolution of these issues. As with actual puzzles and actual onions, there are often many pieces or layers (aspects) that make up the whole, in this case, a particular issue. The more complicated the issue, the more pieces will need to be put into place.

It is possible to have completely cleared one aspect, or even several aspects, and still be left with an unresolved issue, or an issue that continues to recur, despite your best efforts. When an issue seems stubborn, meaning that intensity levels don't seem to go down, or an issue seems to "come back," it is a good idea to explore other aspects of the issue that could still be holding an emotional charge. The aspects of an issue or event can include emotional components, sensory triggers, physiological responses, earlier associated memories, and negative beliefs that support the presenting problem—all of which need to be identified and addressed individually before the issue is truly resolved.

An aspect can be simultaneous, meaning it represents a piece of the event, memory, or trauma you are currently working with; or an aspect can be sequential, meaning it represents a different, compounding event, memory, or trauma. In order to explain each of these, consider an example of an EFT practitioner working with a client on her fear of snakes. Even though the practitioner has spent time addressing the woman's "fear of snakes," some simultaneous aspects the practitioner might consider exploring could be: the way snakes slither, the look of a snake's tongue as it darts in and out of its mouth, the fear of being bitten by a snake, the fear of dying from being bitten by a poisonous snake, and related concerns.

As these aspects are addressed and tapped down to a lower intensity, the practitioner may also encourage the client to begin to think about and explore any potential sequential aspects. An example of a sequential aspect might be an earlier memory of when the client's brother tricked her into putting her hand in a bucket that held a snake and she was bitten. This sequential aspect could have simultaneous aspects of its own, such as the fear she felt when she realized there was a snake in the bucket, the anger and shame she felt when her brother laughed at her, the characteristics of the blood on her hand after she had been bitten, and so on.

Working with aspects can seem overwhelming—any given event, memory, or trauma can hold any number of individual aspects to be addressed—but it can also be very rewarding. Indeed, it is the only way to ensure you have all the parts that impact an event or issue.

In one of Karin's trainings, there was a student who had been afraid of snakes for 45 years, since she was 3 years old. Because Karin was teaching how EFT can work by focusing on aspects, she broke down all the various emotions and triggers for the woman's "fear of snakes." The aspects of her "singular" issue broke down as follows:

- Terrified 10
    - o   It will bite me 10
    - o   It will chase me 9
    - o   I can't move 10
    - o   I could die 9

- Scared 10
    - o   I don't know what to do 8
    - o   Its tail rattles 10
    - o   It slithers 10
    - o   There is nothing I can do 10

- Frozen 10
    - o   If I move, it will bite me 9
    - o   If I move, it will strangle me 8
    - o   I can't run or it will chase me 10
    - o   It's faster than me 10

- Petrified 10
    - o   Its skin is wet 8
    - o   It has scales 9
    - o   It will kill me 9
    - o   I can't move 10

- o It will bite me 10
- o It will strangle me 9
- o It has a forked tongue that comes out 10

Notice that some of the same sub-aspects appear under more than one category. Address these separately. Because all aspects are related, often you will find that the individual intensities of some aspects change as you work with others. Test the levels of intensity as you move through the various aspects. It is often helpful to write down the relative intensity next to each aspect, to provide a record regarding where you began. Marking each aspect before and after treatment ensures that each aspect is addressed, and that each aspect reaches a place of no intensity (or 0 residual distress).

In Karin's demonstration, after 45 minutes of tapping on aspects alone, with no additional wording except what was given by the client, the client was willing to try to touch a snake for the first time in decades. Prior to this, the woman was so afraid of snakes that she had a colleague use contact paper to cover the snake photos in a coursebook before she could even read the training manual.

If you're feeling overwhelmed when working with a stubborn issue that has many aspects, Dr. Patricia Carrington recommends, "Whenever there are multiple aspects and you are uncertain where to start, a good rule of thumb is to start with the earliest memory about the issue and deal with that" (Carrington, 2005–2012a). While this earliest memory will also have its own aspects that need to be addressed in turn, dealing with the earliest memory first can potentially take the charge out of subsequent, sequential aspects.

Your initial work might even resolve the entire presented issue, in the same way that getting to the roots of a weed and loosening the dirt around those roots allows you to easily pull up the entire weed. Aspects are relative in their perceived importance; some aspects may seem larger, or more related to the impact of the memory, than others, and the collapse of one can cause the collapse of others.

Dr. Carrington recommends focusing on one aspect at a time, even if addressing a particular issue in its entirety requires many sessions. She encourages people to keep tapping on one aspect until its relative intensity is at a 2 or below. You might find that treating one aspect of an issue causes other aspects to automatically clear up, or you might not. She states that "there is no need whatsoever to be discouraged when there are many streams to follow when clearing an issue with EFT. What is needed to deal with such a situation is a quiet, steadfast persistence and an awareness that certain things take time" (Carrington, 2005–2012a).

Taking the time to find and identify each of the aspects of a trauma, memory, or event is vital to the success of EFT. We now know that the brain has the unique ability to rewrite memory and readapt it to new learning. This process, referred to as memory extinction or psychological extinction, allows memories to be recalled and contextually altered or preserved. Researchers have identified it as a distinct learning process (Garelick & Storm, 2005). As the aspects of a trauma or event are individually addressed, the brain has the ability to relearn and recategorize issues that might previously have seemed insurmountable. A practitioner's ability to help a client identify and address each aspect of a particular issue is a crucial factor in the success of EFT.

Core Issues

One of the key components to success with EFT, and an area that is helpful to consider when EFT doesn't seem to be working, is identifying and resolving core issues. The information presented in Levels 1 and 2 on core issues and how to identify them can be highly valuable if you find yourself in an EFT session that seems stuck, or when EFT doesn't seem to be working.

Core issues represent the beliefs, perceptions, and decisions we form about ourselves, others, and the world as we go through life. Beliefs are formed from our experiences in life. Many of these were formed in early childhood as we struggled to make sense of events, large and small, that happened to us or that we witnessed. The decisions we make about self, others, and life in general vary considerably from person to person, based on many factors.

Some of the beliefs we form are helpful. For example, as cars on a street can be unpredictable, my mother's admonition to look both ways before you cross the street is useful. Or in getting the message that my mother thinks I can do things well, I come into adulthood believing that I can put forth my best effort with good results most of the time. Other beliefs or perceptions are decidedly not helpful. For example, if my father and others in various ways told me I can't do anything right, and on occasions I've failed to do my assigned task to please the assigner, they were obviously correct: I can't do anything right; I am flawed; I am not good enough. Or the belief could be a reaction: If I don't make waves, I'll be safe; if I don't try, I won't fail; if I blame them and somehow make it their fault, I won't look bad; if I complain enough about how I can't do it, no one will expect anything from me.

Such beliefs, perceptions, and decisions form the foundation of how we react to life and show up in how we approach our life: what we do, what we say and how we say it, what we focus on and what we avoid, and even the relationships we choose. The beliefs, perceptions, and decisions are the core issues behind the presenting problems. These core issues are not always immediately identified by the client or the practitioner, and it requires patience and detective work to uncover the events that built this foundation.

Recall from Level 2 that one of the best ways to begin identifying core issues is to ask exploratory questions. The Level 2 manual provided an extensive list of questions to ask that can help in getting to core issues. The art of asking the right question at the right time takes experience and practice, so it's important to be patient with yourself as you gain the experience necessary to effectively help your clients become aware of their core beliefs.

Remember, all of the wording and information you need for a successful EFT session and for identifying core beliefs comes from within client, even if they cannot immediately access it. Because many core beliefs are formed in childhood, one extremely helpful question when finding core issues is, "When is the first time you can remember feeling that way?"

If, for example, a client came to you because of stage fright, although this person might easily point to several examples of experiencing that fear recently, a better way to begin the process of finding the core issue that led to developing stage fright might be to ask, "When is the first time you can remember feeling that way?" The answer might surprise you—and your client. More often than not, this question is challenging and leads clients to approach the issue from the other side rather than focus on the countless times they can remember having this uncomfortable feeling, or even the most recent time they felt it. The first time your client felt the same fear or anxiety he or she feels on stage might not have occurred on a stage at all.

Karin often reminds her clients throughout a session to tell her whatever pops into their heads first, even if it doesn't seem to fit or make sense. What makes sense on an energetic level (sometimes described as being on a subconscious level) can be very different from what seems to make sense on a conscious level. Encourage your clients to trust their gut, so to speak. Frequently, whatever comes to mind is relevant in some way.

Karin also asks clients how the emotion feels in their bodies and then asks, "When is the first time you can remember feeling that same way in your body?" Be open to whatever comes to mind for your clients, and encourage them to be open as well. People sometimes have "body memories" in addition to word memories. Body memories are recollections or remembrances that appear to be held in the muscles or energy in a part of the body.

For example, Kathryn Sherrod, PhD, described to us a client who could not think of any words related to her memory of a distressing emotion, but she flinched, moving her upper body and head to the left. Later, after tapping on this flinching action, which was actually a reaction to something that happened a long time ago in childhood, this client remembered consciously what she had experienced that created this body memory. Sounds can also arrive in place of words. The client may recall a sound associated with the disturbing emotion. This, too, can provide the basis for resolving issues.

For example, a client came to Karin because her stepfather had often come into her room when she was a young teenager and rubbed her back at night. It was obvious that this was not simply a sign of affection because the stepfather would get an erection. As Karin and her client used EFT to clear the intensities of the various aspects, the client remembered that she would put a metal trashcan at the door so when her stepfather came into her room, it would wake her. She had completely forgotten about that element of the story, and only at that time did she realize where her fear of metal trashcans and dumpsters had originated. Tapping for the associated sound also cleared the fear of metal trashcans.

Sometimes a client might not be able to access childhood memories, or may have difficulty identifying an earlier memory that could be related to the present feeling. In this case, you can invite your client to make it up. Karin calls this approach "Let's Pretend." You can ask clients to imagine an early childhood experience that could have contributed to the current issue. As long as the made-up story is reasonable and believable to clients, it can be as effective as actually having identified a memory. We cover this in more depth later in the book.

Finding core issues can be a challenging process. With experience, you might be able, or believe you are able, to identify a core issue before your client does. Always, always, check with your clients regarding any assumptions about core issues. It is never beneficial to put your clients and their experiences into a box of your expectations. Remember that, as humans, we are more prone to seek evidence to substantiate our beliefs than to seek evidence that might challenge (and possibly disconfirm) our beliefs.

The following is a list of common core-issue themes. As a practitioner, being aware of these themes can be helpful as you begin to identify core issues and beliefs with your clients. Notice these statements often revolve around issues of safety, self-worth, and deservedness:

- I am helpless.
- I am worthless.
- I am unlovable.
- I am dirty.
- There is something wrong with me.
- I am bad.
- Life is supposed to be hard.
- I am supposed to suffer.
- I deserve to suffer.
- Other people don't have life as hard.
- People always leave me.
- I'll never have a decent relationship.
- I'll always be alone.
- The world is always dangerous.
- People cannot be trusted. (Or either men or women cannot be trusted.)
- If people really knew me, they'd think I was horrible.
- I feel like a fraud.
- I am supposed to feel good 100% of the time.
- I can't succeed at anything.

Working to identify and resolve core issues behind one's belief system is a process. Sometimes these key points of information don't reveal themselves right away. Patience and persistence are effective characteristics for us to embrace as we gain experience in energy work.

When a core issue is stated or discovered, ask the client to rate the strength of her belief in her statement. Generally, there are three options for assessing the strength of one's belief, each with its own advantages. Familiarity with the 0-to-10 SUD (subjective units of distress) scale in assessment may make it simple for the client to continue with this measure. An advantage to using the VOC (validity of cognition) scale, which employs a ranking of 1 to 7, with 1 being not at all believable and 7 representing totally believable, is that it gives the client the opportunity to assign a neutral ranking, that is, 4.

Ann's favorite method for assessing limiting beliefs around a core issue is to ask for a percentage of belief, with 100% being totally true and 0 being totally false. The advantage to percentages is that the client may be more willing to start with very small increments to look at a change, such as "I can let go of 3% of my resentment toward my mother" or "I can maybe start to believe that I am at least 5% a worthwhile person."

The type of scale used is less important than the act of measuring the belief so that one can assess progress.

Psychological Reversal

The term "psychological reversal" originated with Roger Callahan and Thought Field Therapy (TFT) when he "noticed that some patients seemed to be unable to benefit from the same interventions that most people found very helpful" (Heitler, 2011). We introduced the idea of Psychological Reversal in the Level 1 training resource book and expanded on it in Level 2. It is still unclear what happens in the energy system when Psychological Reversal (i.e., energy work does not seem to be beneficial) occurs. "One theory is that when a traumatic event depletes your energy to a low level, your energy can become negative." This in turn can elicit the opposite situation to what you would prefer (Gallo, 2000, p. 11).

Though the term has become common throughout the energy-based professions, several organizations have made changes in their explanations of the term. One of these organizations, the Association for Comprehensive Energy Psychology (ACEP), explains Psychological Reversal as involving one's readiness or willingness to resolve issues. According to ACEP, this explanation "may more precisely address the heart of what generates" these seeming reversals (Gruder & Gregory, 2006, p. 2).

Every life change, every decision, every new awareness of a hidden belief system, and every healing carries with it risks and costs. As we change, we risk losing something and gaining something. In addition, many of us fear the "unknown." We might say to ourselves, "I've never done it that way before," "I've never considered that possibility before," or "That won't work for me." Varieties of risks regarding making desired changes have been categorized into different types of Psychological Reversal. For example, the criteria set forth by Fred Gallo (2000), as described in the *EFT Level 2 Comprehensive Training Resource*, include: loss of identity, unwillingness to forgive, deservedness, and safety.

The resistances to change that clients have developed were created for a reason. At one point, those resistances were reasonable or necessary solutions. Those solutions fit the situations in which clients lived at the time they created those solutions. Now, in the clients' current lives, these resistances and old solutions have become part of the problem. Rather than rejecting those resistances and old solutions as representing clients' flaws or limitations that we need to help them get past, we do our clients and ourselves a favor by appreciating that we are endeavoring to help clients apply the same problem-solving skills that they applied earlier in their lives.

To use a computer analogy, what is different now is that we are helping clients give themselves permission to download new, more functional software with more available choices as they replace the outdated, no longer effective, more limited (i.e., rigid) choices and decisions. Sometimes what we are doing is clearing out viruses that have corrupted the software, so the software can work more effectively now.

Though there is still value in the criteria and approaches established by Fred Gallo and his contemporaries regarding Psychological Reversal, the ACEP suggestion that our initial understanding of Psychological Reversal has evolved to accept such reversals as objections to treatment success. These objections can be conceptualized as representing clients' objections to changing until the unintended consequences associated with changing have been clarified and resolved. These objections generally fall into two categories: disorientation fear (DF) and not "understanding" the treatment issue (Gruder, 2006, p. 22). DF is the fear that if treatment succeeds, one's understanding of oneself, others, or how the universe works might be altered in ways that feel scary or undesirable. DF may or may not be a conscious fear. Not understanding the treatment issue simply means that one does not have enough understanding of the issue at hand to tune in to it.

Some practitioners still emphasize Psychological Reversal as a separate issue that must be addressed using specific protocols. Others address resistance to change as if it is just another aspect to be addressed using EFT. No matter how you decide to approach the issues your clients have regarding Psychological Reversal (willingness to succeed, or refusal to move forward until the unintended consequences are addressed), being aware of clients' resistance to change—whether conscious or subconscious—and addressing such issues are valuable to your practice and success as an EFT practitioner.

Resistance to change is a normal reaction to the unknown; there is always a pro and a con to any change. In some ways, we are all resistant; we certainly don't intend to change until we feel it is safe to do so. Though investigative questions and relevant Setups that capture the key issues are often helpful, there are times when it is best not to ask questions. At times it is best to express your desire to learn more in a mildly curious way, with statements such as "Share with me more about what you mean by that."

Pay close attention to the client's language and use EFT to address the conflict, resistance, opposing parts, or type of Psychological Reversal. Be sure to address any additional aspects as needed, and be persistent. Test as you go to make sure your client's concerns and needs are heard and resolved along the way.

Although not generally considered by EFT practitioners, another, perhaps more difficult, "reversal" to consider is Neurologic Disorganization, a concept from applied kinesiology (muscle testing). Neurologic Disorganization represents a more pervasive energy disruption within the body and has been identified in complex physical issues, including neurological problems such as brain injuries or learning disabilities, serious addictive disorders (not cravings), allergies, and ADHD, and when there is a history of an energy psychology method being ineffective. Those trained in applied kinesiology often assess a client's polarity response on every issue. Practitioners have reported that when the client's response to muscle testing is opposite to what would be expected (i.e., a negative response to a positive statement and vice versa) or the responses are the same no matter the question, energy modalities such as EFT may be less effective.

A search of the literature reveals several approaches that have been developed to help resolve pervasive energy disruptions. Most of these are a variation on the Collarbone Breathing process developed by Callahan and originally taught as a part of EFT.

The process as described here may initially appear cumbersome, but once you have practiced it a few times, it is simple to guide your client through the process. You do not need to know muscle testing. Ann uses Collarbone Breathing with any client whose progress is blocked or nonexistent, who is not receiving the benefits generally seen in client sessions, or who comes in reporting having seen other practitioners without success. Use it for yourself as well when you feel blocked.

Collarbone Breathing

The process uses:

- The collarbone points (one inch down and one inch over, on both sides, from the V-shaped notch where a man would tie his tie).
- The pads of the first two fingers of each hand.
- The first two knuckles of each hand.
- The Gamut spot is tapped continuously during each step.
- 5 breathing positions:

o   Take a breath only about *halfway in* and hold 2 seconds.

o   Take a breath as *deeply* as you can and hold for 2 seconds.

o   Let the breath *halfway out* and hold 2 seconds.

o   Let the breath *all the way out* and hold 2 seconds.

o   Breath normally while you switch hand positions.

WITH LEFT HAND

Step 1

a.   Place *left finger pads* on the *left side* collarbone point (cb).

b.   Go through each of the 5 breathing positions, listed above, as you tap the *left hand Gamut spot with right hand fingers continuously throughout each step.*

Step 2

a.   Move *left fingers to right side* cb.

b.   Use the 5 breathing positions while tapping the left hand gamut spot with right hand fingers.

Step 3

a.   Bend *left knuckles* and touch the *left* cb.

b.   Use the 5 breathing positions while tapping the left hand gamut spot with right hand fingers.

Step 4

a.   Move *left knuckles* and touch the *right* side cb.

b.   Use the 5 breathing positions while tapping the left hand gamut spot with right hand fingers.

WITH RIGHT HAND

Step 5

a.   Place *right fingers* on the *left side* cb.

b.   Use the 5 breathing positions while tapping the right hand gamut with left fingers.

Step 6

a.   Move *right fingers* to the *right side* cb.

b.   Use the 5 breathing positions while tapping the right hand gamut spot with left fingers.

Step 7

a.   Bend *right knuckles* on the *left side* cb.

b.   Use the 5 breathing positions while tapping the right hand gamut spot with left fingers.

Step 8

a. Bend *right knuckles* on the *right side* cb.
b. Use the 5 breathing positions while tapping the right hand gamut spot with left fingers.

If your client is driving or responsible for anything important after a session, please make sure that your client is fully grounded and aware before leaving. As an example, Karin was once videotaping an EFT workshop and the sound system was extremely outdated and created a loud irritating buzz. The hotel staff could not correct it. Karin was extremely worried and upset about the situation so she used Collarbone Breathing. As she was doing this, the hotel manager called in a specialist and resolved the problem and the workshop began. As the first speaker began to talk, there was no sound amplification at all. To her own surprise, Karin didn't react at all—not even to fix the problem. Collarbone Breathing had relaxed her to the point of not responding. She forced herself to think and quickly resolved the problem.

The Apex Effect

When considering the process of introducing EFT, it is worth mentioning that there are times when a person experiences dramatic changes through energy work and then does not credit the outcome to the EFT experience. Instead, they find other explanations that make more sense to them, that fit better into their existing belief system. This issue is not only applicable to new EFT practitioners; there are plenty of anecdotes and stories about practitioners whose clients attributed their relief to anything *but* EFT.

Karin Davidson shares a story about a first-time client who came to her early in her practice for relationship help. After working through intense emotional issues and experiencing major shifts throughout the process, Karin checked in with the client and asked how she was feeling. Shrugging, the client reported that she felt different, but since she had been working on these issues with her traditional therapist all along, things must have finally broken through—without the help of EFT.

Karin motioned toward the pile of tissues on the couch next to the client, saying, "See all the tissues you used during this session? You were crying heavily and releasing all through our time together." The client commented that the tissues on the couch were not hers, mentioning how strange it was that Karin would leave another person's tissues there during her session. She left believing that the EFT session had had no effect on her or her issues.

Apex Problem studies have compared the functions of the two hemispheres of the brain to understand this phenomenon. Michael S. Gazzaniga (2012) of Dartmouth College describes the "left brain interpreter" as a built-in set of cognitive functions that create "explanations" for phenomena unfamiliar to it. In other words, when the left brain is presented with something that it does not understand (e.g., the rapid success of EFT), it creates an explanation of its own, even if that explanation is contrary to what has taken place. These rationalizations become so powerful that they override alternative explanations. Remember that what we know and experience is filtered through our brains.

An example of our brains giving us misinformation is "phantom limb pain." In phantom limb pain, people who have lost a hand, arm, or leg, feel pain in the part that is missing. These people know that they cannot really still feel pain in that body part, but the sensation of pain represents an interpretation that occurs in the brain. Sometimes, we believe our brain's interpretations even though our fantastic brains are capable of being in error.

In Karin's blog (Davidson, 2012), she recommends telling clients that the changes they experience may be subtle or that it may be difficult to believe that EFT, essentially "tapping on your face and repeating words," can really be the vehicle of changes so significant that they improve your life. Preframing clients for the possibility that they might experience some version of the Apex Effect can help prevent this. Preframing, in this case, means making clients aware that sometimes people have difficulty believing that such a gentle technique can also be such a powerful technique. You'll learn more about preframing in the next chapter.

Beyond the Basic Recipe: Getting Creative

Part of the beauty of EFT is that the formula remains largely the same even as it is applied to a seemingly endless variety of issues, traumas, and everyday problems. Traditionally, the EFT Setup Statement is "Even though I have *this problem,* I deeply and completely accept myself," with "this problem" replaced by the feeling, movie title, issue, or event on which the client is choosing to focus at the moment.

The Setup has two basic functions. One function is an acknowledgment of the issue, as seen by the client. The actual "truth" of the issue is not relevant. For example, clients might believe they are ugly, worthless, stupid, or unlovable. These are judgments, not truths. Other clients might be focused on having thrown the ball that lost the game, having made an un-signaled turn while driving a vehicle that led to an accident, or having failed an assignment. These are more objective issues. The second function of the Setup is an affirmation or acceptance of self despite having the negative feeling, problem, or issue. Some have stated the structure of the Setup in more therapeutic terms, with the first part being exposure to the problem, and the second part representing a potential cognitive shift into acceptance.

Regardless of how you choose to title the segments of this very important two-part statement, it's all about acceptance. The self-acceptance affirmation in the Setup functions to neutralize or suspend self-judgment and self-rejection, sometimes necessary before real progress can be made. In fact, research has shown that affirmations of personal values "can attenuate perceptions of threat, reduce rumination after failure, and reduce defensive responses to threatening information" (Creswell et al., 2005, p. 846). Through these various steps, affirmations can help buffer the damage potentially created by the stress response. In its most basic form, the Setup is preparing the client for the work they are about to do by tuning them in to the problem or feeling, and helping to create a space of self-acceptance.

Variations on the Setup Statement

There are many variations to the default Setup, "Even though I have *this problem,* I deeply and completely accept myself." Recall in Level 2 that practitioners can use the Extended Setup and the Setup/Reminder Combination to customize the language of the Setup. Some of the ways in which the traditional EFT Setup Statement can be altered are by adding additional information, shifting the focus from a negative to a more positive view (when appropriate), or to reflect the progress made in previous rounds. For example, "Even though I made mistakes as a kid ("as a kid" is additional information), when I want to get things right (a positive expression of the issue), and I *still have some fear* of not being perfect (reflecting progress), I deeply and completely accept myself."

There are several notable EFT variations that employ methods of changing or varying the Setup Statement. One of these variations is Dr. Patricia Carrington's Choices Method, in which the practitioner spends time with clients to formulate the best wording for the clients' choice of the alternative outcome they would like to have for the problem they are addressing. After clarifying the exact wording with the client, the variation to the affirmation is then inserted into the Setup sentence beginning with, "I choose…" (Carrington, 2005–2012b). You can find a complete description of Dr. Carrington's Choices Method in the Level 2 training resource book.

Carrington's Choices Method, as well as others that utilize deviations from the Basic EFT Recipe, rely on sensitivity, timing, and information the practitioner gathers from the client. No matter how practitioners change the wording used with EFT, it is always important to remember to keep it client-driven so the language and concepts remain appropriate for specific clients.

A frequent concern of EFT practitioners involves finding the right words. If the idea of varying the Setup Statement leads you as a practitioner to anxiety or stress, remember that variations are not necessary. EFT works in its most basic form. While getting creative with the Basic Recipe can be an efficient way to move sessions forward quickly, repeating the client's exact words remains important. Attempting to efficiently cover too many aspects in one round carries the danger of skipping over an aspect.

One creative way for developing EFT Setup Statements was utilized by Jasmine Bharathan (2009). Maintaining the idea that the best words come from the client, she recommends having the client draw a tree trunk on a piece of paper. Within the trunk of the tree, have clients write the title of the problem. An example could be: "Angry at Mom." On the left side of the tree, add a branch for each reason for the problem. On each branch, place a leaf with the corresponding feeling. In this example involving anger at Mom, a branch could be: embarrassed me in front of my friends. A leaf on that branch could be: frustration. Another branch could be: showed up unexpectedly. A leaf on that second branch could be: anxiety. On the right side, ask clients to draw a corresponding branch for each one on the left and write in each branch and leaf what would feel better instead. An example for the first branch on the right side could be: independent and loved. An example for the second branch on the right side could be: completely love and accept myself.

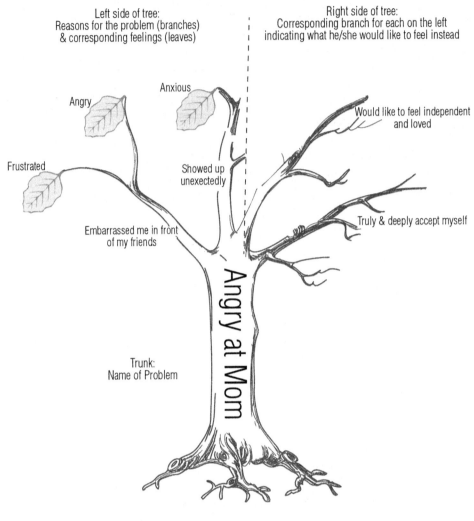

Left side of tree:
Reasons for the problem (branches)
& corresponding feelings (leaves)

Right side of tree:
Corresponding branch for each on the left
indicating what he/she would like to feel instead

Anxious

Angry

Would like to feel independent
and loved

Frustrated

Showed up
unexectedly

Truly & deeply accept myself

Embarrassed me in front
of my friends

Angry at Mom

Trunk:
Name of Problem

"Angry at Mom" Tree

Once the tree is complete, it represents an easy visual formula for custom-made Setup Statements. A statement put together from the example could be: "Even though I'm angry at my mom, and I am frustrated that she embarrassed me in front of my friends, I choose to feel independent and loved." Often, however, until the intensity of the "left side of the tree" has been reduced, clients might not be able to hear or accept their ideal state, for example, being independent and loved.

Another way to address developing Setup Statements is to have clients draw a picture of their problem. Ann suggests that using pictures can be helpful in working with clients who are uncommunicative, out of touch with their feelings, or reluctant to share information. Using pictures works well with children but can be very helpful for adults as well. It can be a helpful exercise for clients to complete and take home to work on themselves. When the picture is drawn, use the client's description of the picture. For instance, the client taps for "that heavy black line" or the "squiggles over the red circle."

Ann used drawing when working with children in a residential treatment facility. Sally was 11, withdrawn and uncommunicative. Ann stopped by her room one day when she had out her crayons. "You look very sad today," Ann said. "Draw me a picture of what the sad looks like." They tapped together for the dark heavy lines, the red squiggles, the blue boy standing all alone, and little "people" in the background. No other words came from Sally; she still had a long way to go to trust anyone. After they had tapped for several minutes, Ann noted Sally's body language relaxing. Ann smiled, turned the paper over, and asked Sally to draw what the sad looked like now. The picture was totally different. Children like Sally rarely resolve their deep issues in one tapping session, but to decrease their internal pain by even two points matters and will often give you the opening for further work.

Talking and Tapping (Ranting)

Beyond the Setup Statement, there is potential for creativity and flexibility within the rest of the Basic Recipe, too. Talking and Tapping, sometimes referred to as Ranting, is a tool that drops the traditional EFT protocol, yet it can be very useful and effective at times. You might find EFT resources in which "talking and tapping" is differentiated from "ranting," while other authors use them interchangeably. For the purpose of this manual, we use them interchangeably because, although the two words might imply a difference in emotional intensity, the approach and application remain the same.

Ranting can be used effectively to clear a great deal of negative emotions in a very short period of time when your client or you are truly tuned in to the emotions. EFT works if you focus on the emotions associated with an issue and tap. By definition, people who are ranting are tuned in to their emotions.

Often clients just need to "vent" as a way of sharing their feelings with someone who will listen with compassion. Tapping through all the points while the client talks, complains, explains, tells a story, cries, yells, or paces around the room can greatly reduce anxiety and stress. For example, you might find yourself with a client who is too overwhelmed by emotion to engage in the traditional EFT protocol. In these types of situations, Ranting can be extremely useful. The basic idea behind Ranting, or Talking and Tapping, is to allow clients to talk, rant, and tell their story while continuously tapping. As long as clients keep tapping, they can significantly decrease their emotional intensity at a relatively fast pace, even though they aren't following a traditional EFT protocol.

Clients do not have to tap on all the points; let them pick and choose. Then too, tapping on only one point can be effective. In these cases, emotions can often be processed just by tapping along with clients while clients are allowed to rant or talk and tap whichever points they wish. The practitioner can encourage clients to continue with occasional comments such as "Yeah!" or "You tell 'em!" or "No way!" or "What else?"

When Ranting is used as an option for clients, you might need to remind them, sometimes more than once, to continue to tap. This is because clients might begin tapping, and then in the excitement or emotion of the rant, they stop. Getting clients to resume tapping can be challenging when they are gesturing with their hands while they tell a story. Interject as often as necessary to remind them to keep tapping. Alternatively, sometimes making eye contact and tapping conspicuously on yourself will help them follow you and do what you're doing. You can also ask questions for additional information (maybe for more specific information), to check on intensity levels, or to direct them to associated memories or events. Encourage clients to be expressive. This is a time when exaggeration and generalization works well. Ranting is not about accuracy; it is about tapping through the storm of emotions as experienced by clients at the moment.

As clients continue in their rant, you might notice their intensity falling, which would lead to their emotions becoming less apparent. The story might even become boring or funny to them as they release and resolve their emotions. They might discover a solution to the problem that had previously eluded them. If a client's perspective changes in a positive and effective cognitive shift, the emotional content of the original story will have significantly decreased. Once the client calms, you will want to address any remaining specific or additional aspects of the original story using the traditional EFT protocol. As in any EFT session, remember to test for intensity levels. It is best to test each part of the rant to make sure you haven't missed any aspects. As you check for any lingering intensity regarding any part of the story, you might discover something else that needs to be addressed.

Karin had a client who was experiencing relationship issues. The woman began her first appointment by speaking very quickly with high emotion, listing all the negative statements her partner had said to her. Instead of stopping her, Karin encouraged her to tap around the points. Karin simply tapped along and listened. The woman was so distressed by her partner's statements that the tapping and talking continued for 40 minutes. No intensity levels were taken and no individual aspects were identified. The woman continued with visible emotions, including anger, guilt, sadness, frustration, desperation, loss, and more. Karin simply kept tapping along with her and nodding her head, listening intently.

Finally, the woman breathed a large sigh and reached for another tissue. She apologized for going on and on, explaining that her emotions had been pent up for a very long time. She paused then, and said, "Oh my, I've been repeating everything he says about me and how it makes me feel...but the truth is, it's his problem—those aren't my thoughts about myself." This cognitive shift of recognizing that those thoughts and words were his thoughts and words, not the client's, occurred through the use of Ranting. The appointment continued with traditional EFT.

Daisy Chains

In EFT, "daisy chaining" is a term used to describe the experience of tapping on one event that leads to another event that, in turn, leads to yet another event. Daisy chains were discussed in the *EFT Level 1 Comprehensive Training Resource.* As explained, you can experience daisy chains when working with yourself or when working with others. They are especially likely to occur when people are Ranting or Tapping and Talking.

As clients move through their presenting story or emotions and as their emotional intensity levels drop, you can ask simple questions to encourage them to move to the next related issue, whether it be another aspect of the presenting event or a different memory altogether. One of the simplest and a surprisingly effective question is "What does this remind you of?" Or, after each round, ask, "What comes up for you now?" Daisy chaining can happen when you allow, or guide, clients from one emotional point to the next while they talk, or rant. As a result, clients then have an opportunity to clear a host of associated memories and emotions at once, while simply tapping and talking.

It is often necessary to remind clients to tell you when other issues, memories, or emotions come to mind. During the rant, or even during a traditional EFT session, the subconscious mind is constantly working at making connections and associations. By virtue of these beliefs, emotions, and conceptualizations being subconscious, clients are not directly aware of them. As these things bubble to the surface, especially when there is a decrease in intensity of a related issue, clients might brush them off as unrelated or unimportant. By asking detailed questions and encouraging clients to be open about things that come up, even if they seem irrelevant to the issue at hand, you can notice daisy chain opportunities.

In addition, as you move through the chain with clients, continue to test for aspects or pieces that may not be entirely resolved or that still hold an emotional charge. Revisiting and addressing these aspects could lead to other daisy chain opportunities. Making a list of events and aspects covered as clients connect experiences through daisy chains that are followed during the session allows you and the client to go back to test that all the aspects and events have been completely addressed.

A potential challenge when using Ranting, Talking and Tapping, or going from one event to the other is that some pieces of the aspects or events can be missed. Even though it might appear that the issue is complete because clients are reporting no residual intensity, possibly expressing a cognitive shift around the issue, go back and thoroughly test the intensity level of all the aspects to make sure everything has been resolved.

Reframing

Reframing is a powerful tool that can be used to help clients change the way they think about a particular issue. We introduced reframing in the *EFT Level 2 Comprehensive Training Resource*. Reframing is an advanced technique, and many people struggle with how and when to reframe. We would like to use this opportunity to offer a short review on the basics of reframing and build on some of the introductory information offered in Level 2.

Tania Prince, one of the founding EFT Masters, offers a useful definition of reframing. She writes that reframing is "the art of linguistically helping a client shift the meaning they give their experiences to a meaning that is more conducive to health and well being and living the life they want to live" (Prince, 2010). Put simply, reframing is based on the idea that each of us gives meaning to our experiences based on our point of view. This means that changing our point of view can change the meaning we assign to a particular memory or event.

An experience only has the meaning each of us personally assigns to it based on previous decisions we have made about others, the world, and ourselves. When we change the meaning we assigned to a particular memory or event, we often change our response, beliefs, or behaviors in response to that memory or event. Consider a painting in a frame. If the painting is displayed in a cheap ugly frame, the painting itself will probably be less appealing. We might even decide that the painting is cheap and awful. The very same painting, when placed in a well-chosen beautiful frame is likely to suddenly have an entirely new look. Even though it is the same painting, it can appear to us to be more beautiful or even of a higher value.

As you have already learned, reframing in EFT was modeled after its use in neuro-linguistic programming (NLP). The concept of helping people shift their views on issues is, however, much older than EFT or NLP. It is a key goal in most therapies.

NLP was developed in the 1970s by Richard Bandler and John Grinder. They studied how highly effective therapists helped people create change in their behavior and their beliefs. One of the methods employed by effective therapists was reframing. Bandler and Grinder developed the Six-Step Reframe Technique, which was introduced in their book *Frogs into Princes* (1979). The concept of reframing has continued to evolve since then.

Though there is no shortage of "steps" and "guides" to effective reframing, it is important to point out that the actual reframing of any situation is up to the client, not the practitioner. Because clients develop a variety of ways to reframe their beliefs, emotions, reactions, and experiences, this text will not cover one specific approach to reframing. Instead, the goal here is to further your understanding of this tool and to offer some general guidelines to consider when helping clients reframe.

The way that we respond to everyday situations is the result of what we believe about the world, others, and ourselves. These beliefs are usually based on the early-life decisions that ultimately shaped the "frame" through which we view the world. Most of our deeply held convictions regarding how people relate to each other and how the world works were developed by the time we were about 6 years old. Surprisingly, as children, we make decisions and determinations that we cling to for the rest of our lives. That is, we cling to them until we stop and reconsider how well our views are working for us. If we notice that they are not working well for us, we have the option of revising them.

Our system of organizing principles and beliefs helps us assess new situations as they happen to and around us. The frame we use guides our mind as it works to evaluate and interpret the things we experience without relying on conscious thought. Based on what we learned and perceived from early life experiences, some of us develop frames that are negative or inaccurate or lead to emotional and behavioral responses that are harmful, painful, or no longer applicable to our current situation.

Most of us have developed frames that are accurate and beneficial in some situations while having blind spots within which our frames work far less well. We can change some of our frames without needing to change all of them. EFT shares this basic concept with several other modalities and traditional approaches, including cognitive behavioral therapy (CBT).

In CBT, reframing is addressed with a technique called cognitive restructuring, in which reason and logic are used to help people become more aware of their cognitions, or "frame." Cognitive behavioral therapists encourage clients to address feelings or beliefs with reality-based questions as part of the reorganization necessary to replace distorted thinking with more accurate and useful thinking. In essence, this approach involves reframing the original belief.

Gestalt therapists help clients become more aware of their ownership of their beliefs, bodily experiences, and emotional reactions as part of making desired changes. That is, clients' awareness of what they are experiencing in the present moment helps them determine if they want to make changes and what types of changes they might want to make (Woldt & Toman, 2005).

In contrast, EFT is focused on balancing clients' energy around the emotions that power or inform their beliefs. When disturbances are cleared, emotions become effective and beneficial rather than being distorted or excessive, so clients can then change their beliefs and related behaviors. By combining tapping with effective reframing, the goal is to help clients shift how they perceive or feel about a particular situation in order to develop a new, more useful response. Conceived and contributed at the appropriate time, reframes can help clients change the meaning of an event or situation, even though the literal facts of the occurrence remain the same. It is not the events or experiences of our lives that create our happiness or our distress. It is our interpretations of what those events or experiences mean about us that lead us to create our happiness or distress.

Skillful and effective reframes are always in clients' best interest. Reframes do not have the purpose of imposing a viewpoint or belief on clients. EFT is client centered; thus reframing, no matter how great a new perspective may seem, is always based on respect for the client. With practice, EFT practitioners can learn to quickly assess clients' current "frame" and use information clients have provided to offer clients opportunities to change their perceptions using additional information that was not previously observed.

Reframes introduced by the practitioner are *not* a necessary part of EFT. Although reframes can encourage cognitive shifts, often aiding or speeding the healing process, EFT alone can resolve all of the emotional aspects of a particular issue and help clients create an internal environment that allows them to change their perceptions and beliefs on their own. Ann suggests that when it comes to reframing, it is always better to be cautious; the best reframes come from an in-depth understanding of clients' current frames of their world. Reframes that are premature or that come from the practitioner's belief system or agenda can slow or stop a session and can also interfere with your rapport with the client.

When it comes to effective reframing with a client, perhaps the practitioner's most critical role is to identify the client's current "frame" and help the client identify and resolve all of the aspects and emotions around the issues comprising that frame. As a general rule of thumb, once the client's current "frame" has been identified, its intensity should be decreased before the reframe is introduced. After all, if you are highly emotional, it is difficult for you to take in new cognitions. If, for your testing method, you are utilizing the subjective units of distress (SUD) scale, which is a commonly utilized intensity rating, make sure that the client's emotional intensity is 3 or less before introducing a reframe.

Note: The subjective units of distress scale, credited to Joseph Wolpe in 1969, is one example of a self-anchored scale that uses numbers to equate the intensity of one's thoughts and feelings: the *subjective* distress a client may be experiencing. Wolpe's original self-anchored scale ranged from 0 to 100 subjective units of distress (SUD); however, a 0–10 scale is most commonly used in EFT. You can find more information on other self-anchored scales. It is not necessary to teach your client the technical name of this or any scale, or review with your client what each level of distress would represent. Simply asking, "On a scale of 0 to 10, where would you rank the feeling you are having right now?" will suffice.

Reframes can be used in some situations at the beginning of a session, most often to help clients reach a place of acceptance of themselves and their issues. The goal here is to work around resistance to using a personal affirmation in the Setup Statement or resistance to addressing the issues by helping the client recognize a strength already exhibited or an obvious choice he or she has not yet recognized. For example, a client who is afraid of addressing a particular event might be gently encouraged by: "Even though I don't want to look at this event because I am afraid, I can work at my own pace and I can remember that I control how fast or deep I go." Likewise, a client who feels overwhelmed and doesn't know where to begin might benefit from: "Even though I have too many problems to know where to start, I have already taken the first step by trying EFT in the first place and recognize I don't have to see all the rest of the steps to move forward."

These gentle reframes are not addressing a specific event and are not following the "decrease the intensity" rule, but can be effective tools in establishing rapport and creating an environment of safety that is conducive to the client being able to move forward in the healing process. Even these gentle introductory reframes should be checked with the client to determine whether they fit the client's belief system at the moment. If the reframe of recognition of their strength or choice does not "land," ask the client what would fit.

On the occasional times when clients are not willing to give themselves credit for taking the first step toward solving the problem, or any other reframe that recognizes an existing strength or choice, Ann forms a gentle question that asks, "What are you willing to give yourself credit for?" If they cannot find anything for which they are comfortable accepting credit, you have already uncovered a core issue.

There is an art to effective delivery of reframes to a client. Some general rules to keep in mind are:

- Effective reframing is built on rapport and trust. It will be next to impossible to offer a good reframe to a client with whom you have neither and who does not feel safe in the therapeutic space. Meet your clients where they are in the immediate moment in the session with you and do the trust-building work that can be imperative to creating a positive client-practitioner relationship.

- Reframing relies on communication. You must first gather enough information about the client's presenting issue and find a specific event related to it. Use words and phrases from clients to create Setup Statements they are comfortable with to continue to develop rapport and begin to address the emotions around the issue.

- Reframes are generally most effective when the client has an intensity level of 3 or less. If the intensity remains above a 3, there is more work to be done or more aspects to be addressed before clients are likely to be comfortable with reframes. That is, while clients' intensity levels are above a 3, they are likely still stuck in their issues. Only when their intensity levels drop to a 3 or below, have they gotten themselves unstuck enough to be capable of viewing things from a different perspective.

- Listen closely to how the client frames the current issue and, when the intensity is at an appropriate lower level, offer a well-timed alternative that might make sense to the client. Develop a Setup phrase that acknowledges the issue and use a reframe in place of the typical acceptance statement.

- Not all reframes will "stick" or "land" with the client, even if they appear to be well stated or well timed. This is not the end of the world. Remember that reframing is actually up to the *client*, not the practitioner, so a reframe that doesn't work simply indicates that the client wasn't ready or the words weren't right. Check with the client to gauge the appropriateness of a reframe. You might ask, "Does that fit?" or "Is that right?" "Is there a better way to say that?" Reframes are always *offered*, never imposed. If the reframe didn't land, you can cover your tracks, so to speak, by adding "waffle words" such as "maybe," "someday," "I wonder if it's possible," "that's not true for me," or "when I'm ready" and simply move on. These types of phrases can help clients feel comfortable in accepting or rejecting reframes and avoid breaking rapport. The client's reaction to an ineffective reframe provides feedback, that is, additional information to work with. Sometimes reframes that are not accepted at the moment provide food for thought or are a way of planting seeds that clients might consider over time.

- Another aspect related to reframes is for practitioners to pay attention to reframes *they* might want clients to make. Any time practitioners notice that they have a reframe in mind for a client, it is possible that they have uncovered issues of their own to resolve. That is, the more we believe we know what other people need to be thinking, feeling, or believing, the more work we have to do to realize that our job is not to tell other people how to live their lives. Our job is to help clients get out of their own way so they can move in the directions they want to move in.

Conservative and Bold Reframes

Generally speaking, reframes can be divided into two groups. You may come across some resources that refer to "content reframing" and "context reframing." Content reframing refers to *changing the meaning a situation or event holds,* while context reframing refers to *changing the context of one's view,* or the perspective from which one is viewing the situation. An example of content reframing could come from a woman whose mother never spoke positively about her father who no longer lived in their home. Before reframing the content of the situation, she might have been resentful that her mother never had anything nice to say about her dad: "She just didn't like men, and tried to get me to feel the same way." An example of a content reframe could be the realization that her mother was actually trying to protect her from feeling disappointed in her father's inconsistency and inability to be present by being honest about the situation. Here, the meaning the experience held for the individual has changed—the situation was still the same, but instead of feeling like her mother was trying to convince her to hate men, she is now able to see that her mother was trying to keep her from feeling disappointed or hurt.

An example of context reframing could come from a client who felt guilty for her parents' divorce. A shift in perspective from a 6-year-old girl who blamed herself to that of an adult who knows that divorce is never a 6-year-old's fault could represent an important contextual reframe.

In EFT, we recognize that these two types of reframing seem interchangeable and often occur hand in hand. Other approaches differentiate them. For the purpose of using reframes with EFT, we will categorize them differently, dividing them into two types: conservative reframes and bold reframes.

A conservative reframe refers to a statement that will most likely be easy for the client to accept and integrate. These are often relatively generic statements that might seem obvious to practitioners but have not yet been considered, or adopted, by the client. Examples of these types of reframes include:

- I didn't know any different at the time.

- That was then and this is now.

- I learned that lesson really well when I was 5, but I have better resources to choose from now.

- Even though it was awful when that happened, I survived.

- Maybe they were doing the best they could at the time.

Conservative reframes often involve gently stating the obvious. For instance, in one of Ann's classes, the "client" was dealing with weight issues and brought up a specific event as a young child in which her parents were giving her a lecture about being overweight. After dealing with the aspects of the event, when the intensity was low, the student practitioner made the reframe, "Even though my parents were lecturing me, again, about my weight, it was they who were feeding me." The client began to laugh and her intensity went to a 0. When the event was tested the next day, the intensity remained at a 0.

As always, check reframe wording with the client, even with conservative reframes, to see whether a particular reframe landed. Sometimes you will be able to tell the success of a reframe by observing the client's body language; they might smile, laugh, nod, or roll their eyes. Watch closely because some clients may not feel comfortable enough to tell you whether a reframe fit or not. Others will express their opinions if prompted by the practitioner.

Bold reframes are more challenging for clients to accept because bolder reframes require a bigger shift in perception. As always, proceed with caution and pay attention to where your client is. Timing of reframes is essential for reframes to land. Some examples of bold reframes are:

- **Identifying patterns.** A reframe can provide insight into parallels between current events and other times when the client experienced similar emotions or behaviors. This approach is useful when a client is reluctant to let something go. For example, "Even though I shut down when my wife criticizes me, I recognize that it reminds me of how I felt when my mother scolded me as a child."

- **Forgiveness.** When the emotions surrounding a memory or event are down to 0, forgiveness, when appropriate, often happens naturally. A reframe can introduce the perspective of the offending party from an objective or compassionate perspective. A reframe could allow a greater understanding of one's own behavior in a particular situation. A word of caution: When introducing any concept of forgiveness, it is important to know what the word "forgiveness" means to the client. Forcing or simply introducing forgiveness before a client is ready can damage rapport. An example of an appropriate reframe for forgiveness might be, "Even though she wasn't there for me the way I would have liked her to be, I realize that she was probably just as overwhelmed by the situation as I was." You may want to check to see if your clients erroneously believe that forgiveness means making whatever happened "okay." We don't have to forgive things that are okay. We forgive things that were definitely *not* okay.

- **Humor.** Humor as a reframing tool was discussed in Level 2. You already know that humor can be an incredibly powerful tool in EFT when used appropriately. If a client is ready, pointing out the humor or inherent conflicts within a belief or perception can be an effective reframe. Sometimes connecting with the absurdity of a particular belief can foster a significant cognitive shift. Again, use caution. If not timed correctly or based in strong rapport, using humor in a session can backfire. An example of using humor in a reframe is "I react to my father the same way now as when I was 7; all the best relationship advice comes from 7-year-olds."

Progressive Reframing

There is often a progression in introducing a reframe into a session. For example, a client may come to work on an issue and, while consciously saying they would like to be free of the issue, there is subconscious (sometimes even conscious) resistance to letting go of a difficult emotion or event. These reasons could include secondary gains, fear of change, or discomfort around losing a familiar coping skill, among others. One way to progressively introduce reframing with tapping words could be:

- Karate Chop (KC) point: Even though I want to let go of this anger toward my brother, there's a part of me that thinks he'll get away with it if I do.
- KC: Even though I want to let this anger go, I'm not ready to and you can't make me.
- KC: Even though this anger is hurting me, my brother deserves to have my anger.
- Tapping around the points
  - o You can't make me let this go.
  - o I can't make me let this go.
  - o Nobody can make me let this go.

- o   Until I'm good and ready and I'll never be good and ready.
- o   If I let this go, he'll get away with it.
- o   It doesn't matter how tired I am of carrying this around.
- o   I refuse to let this go.

Check with your client about the wording and what may have "hit home" before going on to the next step, as you support the client in moving toward wanting to let go.

- • KC: Even though I'll never let this go, maybe I'm tired of all this.

- • KC: Even though I refuse to let EFT help me, I wish this didn't hurt me so much all the time.

- • KC: Even though I'll never forgive him, maybe I'd like to stop hurting so much.

- • Tapping points
  - o   I'm tired of carrying this around.
  - o   I'm tired of holding this anger and it not making my brother change.
  - o   I'll never let him get away with this, but I wonder if it's possible that my anger is hurting me more than him.
  - o   Maybe I can let this go when I'm good and ready, but I don't think I'll ever be good and ready.
  - o   Yes I do.
  - o   No I don't.
  - o   Yes I do.
  - o   No I don't.
  - o   Maybe I can let it go from me and it's all still his fault.

This approach recognizes and addressed the conflict between wanting to and not wanting to let this go. Examples of even stronger reframing statements would be:

- • KC: Even though this is all his fault and I'll never let him off the hook, I'm tired of carrying this around and choose now to let it go.

- • KC: Even though I'll never forgive him, this anger is hurting me more than him and I'll show him by letting it go from me.

- • KC: Even though I've carried this around for years, I now choose to know that he doesn't deserve to hurt me all the time and I'm willing to let the anger go as long as I still know it's his fault.

- • Tapping points:
  - o   I'm tired of carrying this around.
  - o   He doesn't deserve for me to hurt like this.
  - o   I'll show him, I'll just let the pain go.
  - o   Even if I don't forgive him, I won't let him get under my skin anymore.
  - o   I wonder if it's possible that he was just reacting.

o   And I'm not going to bother letting it get to me anymore.

o   It's not my job to fix him.

o   It's not my job to be his mother or his wife.

o   I can take care of myself instead and not make myself convince him that it's his problem and not mine.

In reframing, timing is everything. Pay close attention to the client's existing "frame," words, and physiology. Reframes are always offered; if the client doesn't accept your offering, gather more information before offering again.

In summary, reframing is a powerful tool that can be used in conjunction with EFT to foster cognitive shifts that stick. It is important to remember that good reframing is always respectful to clients and where they are now, so it is based in strong rapport and communication. The actual reframing of any situation is up to the client, not the practitioner. As a practitioner, you can release any pressure you feel about having to "make" a reframe happen. Listen to the client, ascertain their current "frame," tap for the intensity around the memory or event first, and then, if appropriate and if the client is ready, carefully introduce a reframe.

Some effective reframes are spontaneous and seem to come from the practitioner's intuitive sense. This intuitive sense is better developed when we also develop the ability to "get out of our own way," which is best accomplished by doing our own work, dealing with our own issues so they don't interfere while we're working with others, and much practice with multiple clients in listening to and trusting our own internal guidance. Don't overthink; remember, reframes are not critical to the success of EFT. It is perfectly acceptable—advisable, even—to hone your skills at using EFT alone before attempting to add reframes.

Perspective and Denial

When reading about reframing in this book and the *EFT Level 2 Comprehensive Training Resource,* you may have noticed a trend. As previously iterated, reframes come from the client, not the practitioner. As a practitioner, it is not your job to "make" the client accept a reframe, and it is not even your job to "invent" the best or the right reframe. Clients will come to reframing naturally after working through the event, whether or not you are able to offer it to them.

Some practitioners struggle with the concept that the client does the internal reframing and, when a practitioner does offer a reframe, *it is the client's prerogative to accept or deny the offered reframe.* This can be a challenge for practitioners who believe that they can see the "right" path to the end of the session or know what the client needs. Although there are ways of intuiting information within the context of a session, which will be discussed later in this book, it is the client's perspective and personal insights that create change with EFT.

While teaching a Level 3 workshop, Karin had a student who was trained as a traditional therapist and relied heavily on her learned understanding of people to offer solutions and move forward in EFT sessions. We will call her Diane. Karin teaches that the answers lie within clients, with their wording and perception, and not in the practitioner trying to figure out what is "wrong" with the client or trying to impose a particular "path." There is value in developing counseling skills, which are especially useful in therapy sessions. From an EFT perspective, however, practitioners pay attention to the process while remaining aware that clients have their own unique perspective on everything they experience. This means that clients might well perceive things differently from the way their practitioner does. Alternatively, sometimes clients might agree with their practitioner, which could sometimes lead them both to notice the same things and miss the same things. In order to illustrate this concept to the class, Karin incorporated an exercise.

Students were paired and one was asked to choose something in the room. The partner was instructed to ask questions to try to figure out the chosen object, with the partner only answering yes or no to the questions. Because of the odd number of students in the class, Karin and Diane ended up as partners. Diane was confident she was "great at this kind of stuff" and heavily relied on her ability to understand what people in sessions with her needed. Diane commented, "This is what I'm good at. We'll be done in no time."

The exercise continued until every other person in the room was finished, with only Diane and Karin remaining. Diane seemed extremely frustrated and surprised that she was not finding what the object was. Finally, she said, "What the heck is it? I really don't know and everyone else is finished." Karin told her it was the workshop coordinator's nametag lanyard.

Diane responded immediately, "But that's not black! When I asked you if the color of the object was intense, you said yes!" Karin explained that the lanyard is bright teal and that bright teal is intense in her opinion. It was the perfect illustration of differing perspectives. To one person, the word "intense" signified "black," and to another, it signified "bright." Neither was correct from an objective perspective and neither was wrong. The light bulb went on over Diane's head. She understood that her own interpretations of words could hinder her ability to move forward objectively. As practitioners, all of us can fall into the same trap with our clients.

When it comes to reframing, intuition, and working with clients in general, it is essential to remember that we forge our interpretations from our histories, knowledge, and culture, and our own ways of handling situations that we experience. Our interpretations might not line up with the interpretations of our clients, so we cannot lead clients where we think they ought to go. The information, direction, reframes, and, ultimately, the resolutions in a session will all come from the client.

EFT Master Gwyneth Moss often uses the analogy of EFT practitioners being like guide dogs (seeing-eye dogs). "It's not the guide dog's job to decide where to go: it's the guide dog's job to get across the roads safely" (Moss, 2010). A guide dog does not push or pull its owner anywhere; it does not force its own agenda. Rather, it ensures the individual's safety, helps when necessary, and it always in tune with its master's (client's) needs. As EFT practitioners, we can learn a lot from guide dogs.

Preframes

In a similar vein, preframing can help set the context for the next phase of the EFT work and support positive expectations for change (Church, 2013b, pp. 277–278). In other words, just as reframes can help shift the frame through which a client views a particular situation or event, a preframe, that is, explaining what to expect or clarifying existing expectations, can help manage perceptions in a way that provides preparation and guidance before a new experience when that new experience does not have an existing frame. A preframe sets the stage for a new experience.

Imagine that you are talking on the phone with a good friend. You mention that you have plans to try a new restaurant later that week. To your surprise, your friend responds by saying, "That place is awful! John and I went there a few weeks ago and the service was lousy and they couldn't even get my order right! We would have been better off having dinner at home." Even though you have not personally had an experience with the restaurant in question, if you go there, you will be prepared to be disappointed. You might even be likely to look for negative qualities about the restaurant and your experience there¬ because your friend preframed your experience. On the other hand, if your friend had reacted positively and raved about the food, the service, and the atmosphere, you would probably be more likely to visit the restaurant expecting to have a fantastic meal.

Just as you can use preframes intentionally to set the stage for a successful experience with EFT, you can also preframe common difficulties that clients could encounter in the course of their EFT work. For example, you can help clients frame their view of progress with EFT by reminding them that changes can be subtle, especially with larger issues, or that the changes experienced after a session can be unexpected or seem unrelated to the focus of the session. Remember that some clients need more information than others to feel comfortable; preframing the entire EFT experience does not need to happen all at once. It will more likely be an ongoing process in which information is added and even repeated.

One of the aspects of EFT sessions that might be difficult for clients is the prospect of recalling early childhood memories. To make matters worse, clients often come with the erroneous perception that they have to somehow remember the "right" memory for each particular issue. Preframing what to expect and what may happen can circumvent this.

For instance, when working with clients to identify an earlier memory or remember the first time they experienced something, you can preframe with, "Just tell me the first thing that pops into your head, even if you don't understand it or it doesn't seem to be related or make sense. It's okay if you can't remember anything specific. Many people have trouble with this now and again; we have ways of working around it." This way, as clients go into the process of remembering specific events, they can do so without the added pressure of remembering the "right" thing or having to understand why it may or may not be related to the issue at hand,

and that it's okay if they have only partial or even no memories. We invite clients to relax. Approaching situations with this preframe actually encourages clients to provide more effective answers and supports them in recalling specific memories. It also builds rapport and encourages more open communication throughout the rest of the session.

This is just one example of how preframes can be used to promote success in EFT sessions, with new and existing clients alike. Some other areas in which you might find preframing useful are:

- Energy disruption and meridians.

- The importance of specific events and "first time" memories.

- Core issues.

- The generalization effect.

- The Apex Effect

- Techniques for approaching especially difficult or painful situations and issues without having to discuss the issue or share all of the related information (e.g., Tearless Trauma Technique).

- Expected results and side effects, such as feeling tired after a session or heightened distress as issues are addressed and emotional layers are addressed and resolved.

- Unrealistic expectations around results (e.g., when a client has seen a "one-minute wonder" somewhere else and expects the same outcome).

With effective preframing, you can help ensure a more successful experience with EFT for clients. You can also prevent some of the misunderstandings and misconceptions that lead people to believe that EFT is ineffective.

Tools for Building Bridges

Often the first step to using EFT is figuring out how to introduce it to friends, family members, and clients who have no working knowledge of what EFT is or how it works. Some people have simply labeled it absurd. The easiest way to help someone be open to the concept that EFT is a viable and effective method is to ask them to try it, perhaps on an issue as simple as the depth of their current breath. There is often a great chasm between an individual's belief system and the way EFT looks and sounds. This can be especially true when it comes to tapping on more serious issues, such as emotional trauma or physical illness. How do you help a person move from one side of the disbelief chasm to the other?

You build a bridge. "Building Bridges simply means helping your client make emotional and intellectual connections from something with which they are familiar, to this unusual looking/sounding new [technique], EFT" (Look, 2010). Helping others connect things that are already familiar with something that is unfamiliar can play an important role in helping potential clients take the first step toward trying EFT. Effective bridges will improve your ability to spread the word about what you do and communicate the benefits of this highly beneficial technique. Making a connection between the known and unknown helps people feel comfortable with the concept of EFT and can play an important role in building rapport with a new or potential client. The concept of Building Bridges is similar to building rapport, which is an important process that you are, it is hoped, already aware of when connecting with clients.

Whether you are introducing EFT in a situation that requires a 30-second elevator speech or you find yourself with the luxury of ample time, there are a variety of tools you can use in your introductions to help build bridges to believability.

Describe Your Own Experience

Most people are swayed by the experience of people whom they trust. If you describe the benefits you have obtained from using EFT along with the specifics you experienced, you provide opportunities for people to ask further questions about your experience, including why you tried this relatively novel approach. Your enthusiasm regarding your experiences is likely to be contagious and often encourages people to want to try this approach.

Establish Credibility

For people with little experience with EFT, you can establish credibility by directing people to articles, research, resources, videos, or quotes about how and why EFT works. These sources sometimes provide the extra push into believability a person may need to be willing to try it for him or herself. Written resources can alleviate misconceptions people have about EFT or energy modalities in general. There are a multitude of established and credible EFT resources to choose from, including an ever-growing library of EFT research via outcome studies, double-blind experiments, and clinical trials. Many of these resources have been conveniently compiled at Research.EFTuniverse.com.

Make Connections with the Known

Though research articles and studies can go a long way in establishing credibility for someone who is skeptical of EFT, not everyone will regard these sources as influential. Some people have no interest in such clinical resources, and others may not be in the position to access or read them. Your goal is to help people make connections between EFT and something they already understand. For example, because most people have heard of or have possibly had experience with acupuncture, you could draw a parallel between the two, connecting the unknown, EFT, to the known, acupuncture. You could say that EFT has been called "emotional acupuncture" and that it employs touch instead of needles.

During introductory sessions, either with individuals or groups, Ann Adams often mentions the fact that people use touch for comfort all the time, even without realizing it. For instance, when stressed, people might press their fingers to their temples, squeeze the bridge of their nose, or place their hand on their chest. She writes:

> I tell them that the amazing part of what they are about to learn [EFT] is not that it works—we already know that touching our body makes us feel better—but that we can consciously focus on an issue we would like to resolve and consciously use a sequence of touches or taps to make us feel better about that issue!

There are countless examples of introductory statements that can help people feel more comfortable with EFT by making a connection with something with which they are already familiar. One practitioner paired chocolate and EFT. "I've heard that eating a lot of chocolate can make your brain feel the same as being in love. Apparently, chocolate changes your energy and emotions. When we tap on acupressure points, EFT changes our energy and our emotions about bothersome people or negative events—and no calories."

The trick is finding what works for your audience, whether acupuncture, the power of touch, chocolate, or something entirely different.

Introduce EFT Through Experience

Often the most effective way to present EFT is to offer people an opportunity to experience it and form their own opinion about EFT. Personal experiences are invaluable. Remember that an introductory experience like this is the time to work on something small and easily measurable. Introductory experiences are intended to provide interested people with opportunities to appreciate the gentle power of this technique.

In short introductory trainings, depending on the amount of time available, Ann may use the Constricted Breathing exercise, a physical discomfort, a craving, a scene from a movie, book, or TV show, or an annoyance in the participant's life that when focused on still brings an emotional response. These less complex approaches still allow the audience to experience the impact of EFT without opening up painful emotional issues you may not have time to complete. In other words, avoid choosing a person's deepest, darkest, secret trauma for an introductory experience. Help your audience pick something that is a very short event and is very specific.

Nonetheless, it's important to be aware that one of the challenges of opening up someone's emotional issues is that you never really know where it will lead. It's always best not to go where you don't belong. All therapists and practitioners have limits to their experience and knowledge. They recognize that there are issues and scenarios for which they are not qualified or trained. This means that they know when to refer clients to someone who is trained and experienced in handling those concerns.

Not going where you don't belong also means not going into issues and scenarios for which you have not built the relationship or established the rapport that would enable you to address them safely and effectively. Consider whether you have the available time to follow something through to completion. As even a "small" issue can be connected to something much larger and more involved, some experts suggest using the simple technique of Constricted Breathing to help both newcomers to EFT and skeptics experience measurable and noticeable results without delving into deeper issues (Schecter, 2013). You may already be familiar with this method, but it is useful in so many situations that it is reviewed here.

Constricted Breathing Technique

1. Slowly inhale two or three deep breaths. This will open the airways and stretch out the lungs, so that any improvement after EFT cannot be attributed to the normal stretching of the lungs.

2. Now, take another deep breath. This time, assess the depth of breath on a scale of 0 to 10, with 10 representing the lung's maximum capacity. Do several rounds of EFT, assessing depth of breath between each round and noting any changes. Use Setup phrases such as "Even though I have constricted breathing…" and "Even though I can only fill my lungs to an 8…" and so on. Or simply, "Even though I'm not breathing to my full capacity…" Then tap several times around the points using simple Reminder Phrases such as "It's an 8" or "I'm not breathing to my full capacity." Generally, there will be noticeable improvement in the depth of your breath when you stop to test.

3. You can take the Constricted Breathing Technique a step further by exploring any emotions or memories that come up during the exercise. For some, the constriction of breath brings up a memory of another feeling or time, or there could be an emotional cause to the constriction, such as anxiety.

There are myriad ways to introduce EFT to those who are unfamiliar with it. Whether you find yourself with only a few moments of someone's time and are able to utilize a confident, concise elevator speech, or you have the opportunity to work with someone as they experience EFT for the first time, the key is understanding your audience and which elements of your expertise and experience can help you build a bridge from EFT to where they are. You also may come across people who are not open to EFT or other energy modalities and who do not want to try your "awesome new thing." This is entirely their prerogative and, as professionals, we respect others' boundaries and preferences.

Using Metaphors

A significant part of using creative language occurs in the form of metaphors. A metaphor is a transfer of symbol, or, according to the *Merriam Webster* dictionary, "a figure of speech in which a word or phrase literally denoting one kind of object or idea is used in place of another to suggest likeness or analogy between them." Linguistically, and in the case of most models, including EFT, metaphor is defined more broadly as any figurative language, including similes, puns, analogies, idioms, anecdotes, and any figurative stories that have multiple interpretive meanings (Ehrnstrom, 2011).

Skilled practitioners usually have multiple approaches and tools at their disposal because what works with one client or situation might not work with another. Metaphors are helpful because they provide another tool to use with a variety of clients and can prove a valuable addition to your toolbox of approaches.

One of the primary reasons that metaphors can be a valuable tool when used with EFT is that they offer an indirect path to addressing a particular issue or event that can be gentle and subtle. In this sense, metaphors provide a mechanism through which clients can explore issues while maintaining distance from them. They can control the depth at which they choose to explore. "Like the sugar that makes the medicine go down, the use of metaphor helps clients tolerate the unpleasantness that they may experience on the journey to self-knowledge" (Loue, 2008, p. xii). For example, a client struggling with a particularly painful or difficult memory might benefit from a protective metaphoric distance, allowing them to work on issues gently and yet effectively.

In one session, Ann was working with a client concerning his extreme anxiety around eating in front of others. He realized this problem stemmed from experiences in his childhood home; however, as he considered events, he became agitated and distressed. In order to create some protective distance from his high emotions, Ann remarked it might be useful to simply picture where in his home this anxiety "lived" rather than continue to find a specific event right now. With only a moment's hesitation, he replied, "The basement. It's like a monster in the basement."

From that point forward, they addressed his anxiety issue as "the monster in the basement." He was able to imagine approaching the anxiety issue in the context of his childhood home by opening the basement door, walking down one or two steps, and addressing the feelings and information that came up from the imagined proximity. In his visualization, he was able to back up a number of stairs, close the door, or even walk to another place in the house if the "monster" became too big or too overwhelming. In this case, the use of metaphor allowed the client to have control over his approach to the issue, which allowed him to connect to it in a way that was significantly more effective than the attempts at approaching the issue directly had been.

As with many EFT tools and modalities, remember that the most valuable information in any session comes from the client. Metaphors are profound because they do not push clients to take on a new perspective. Metaphors allow clients to explore an issue without committing to a viewpoint or deciding to apply a suggested metaphor to their own situation until they have changed and developed it to a point that it works for them.

In the example with the client and his anxiety around eating, Ann offered an option without any vested interest in how, or whether, he chose to use or interpret it. Because the issue was around eating, she could have assumed that the metaphor for his anxiety was the kitchen or the table in his childhood home; instead, she offered an option that prompted a metaphor. This allowed him to develop his visualization into something that accurately represented what he was feeling and experiencing. From that vivid visualization, he created the content of the metaphor. He could have chosen not to take the offered avenue at all. His response could have been, "I am afraid of a monster, but it doesn't live in my childhood home; it lives in my gut." Regardless of how he chose to respond, his response would offer additional information and guidance regarding which direction would be reasonable for to him to take as he resolved his issue. A choice that would be best for him might be viewed as irrelevant by another client.

Clients sometimes spontaneously use metaphors to communicate what's going on for them and what they are feeling. Since metaphors and figurative language can evoke a range of verbal and sensory associations, many people use them to describe and communicate things that are otherwise abstract to them. Using metaphors to describe experience is common in everyday language. How many times have you heard someone say, "I have butterflies in my stomach," "My head is pounding," "My heart is broken," "She's as blind as a bat," or "There are pins and needles in my foot"? Metaphors are an important part of our day-to-day language, and can provide vital information in the context of an EFT session.

When conducting a session, pay attention to these "metaphoric kernel statements" (Fernandez, 1977; Witztum, van der Hart, & Friedman, 1988) that clients sometimes use to communicate important information. Fernandez (1977) referred to these statements as "metaphoric kernel statements" because they are figurative in nature (metaphoric) and communicate something essential (kernel statements). When clients offer these kernel statements, you can tap directly on the information they provide, or help them develop the metaphor further to gather more information and more details.

For instance, someone might describe their inability to focus at work by saying, "It's like my mind runs in 100 different directions, and I can focus on everything but work." In this case, the metaphoric kernel statement would be "my mind runs in 100 different directions." You could begin by tapping on that information, or ask your client to develop the metaphor further: Where does your mind run? What is your mind running from? When does this most happen? When else can you remember feeling this way? You could also say, "Share more with me what that is like for you."

The descriptive metaphoric statements can be an important way for your clients to communicate abstract feelings to you. Within these statements, they might provide significant and tappable information and images with which to work.

Physical symptoms and pain are also prime areas for the use of metaphors, for both client and practitioner. Clients may use imagery and metaphors to describe their physical symptoms, for example, "There's a weight on my chest" or "The pain in my back is stabbing like a knife." As a practitioner, you can encourage your clients to use metaphor to describe and approach their pain or physical symptoms. Use questions like:

- What does that pain feel like?
- If your pain had a shape or a size, what would it be?
- If the pain had a color, what would it be?

- What does this pain look like?
- If this pain were an object, what would it be?

These types of questions can help clients generate additional information about something they may ordinarily have difficulty grasping or describing. Paul Lynch, one of the original EFT Masters, uses an entirely metaphoric technique for approaching pain and physical symptoms in his Color of Pain technique (described in the *EFT Level 2 Comprehensive Training Resource*). If your clients have difficulty applying physical and metaphoric attributes to their pain, encourage them to "just guess." In most cases, the subconscious will provide the pertinent information. There is no right or wrong answer; it is all simply information you could use.

What does it mean to say that the subconscious will provide pertinent information? The idea that the subconscious has information that it will share with the conscious mind is the basis for believing that we reveal ourselves when we make a "slip of the tongue." That is, we might have meant to say one thing, but instead we said something else. Sometimes these "slips" represent the subconscious mind trying to get our conscious attention to recognize something that the subconscious mind has been aware of for a while. Similarly, when we bypass our conscious mind, guessing rather than stating facts, the things we guess are usually prompted by our subconscious mind.

At times, clients have guessed the age they might have been when something happened during their childhood, and then had a family member verify that guess. Clients have also guessed regarding an event in the family that was never mentioned, only to discover that the event actually did happen. Sometimes clients guess at what may have motivated the actions of another person, eventually becoming aware that they too are responsive to that type of motivation.

Not only can metaphors provide pathways to additional information and tappable imagery, they can also be a highly accessible way to measure progress and success with EFT. "When changes occur, these statements [metaphoric kernel statements] are also modified, becoming indicators of therapeutic progress" (Witztum, van der Hart, & Friedman, 1988, p. 3). In the case of physical issues, you can check in with the imagery provided to see how it has changed. This can be done solely through modifications in the description or by applying a 0–10 scale to estimate the intensity of the original image, or both.

For example, if you begin tapping on your client's "red ball of anger" that is located in the stomach, you can check in by asking how the red ball has changed or moved, or you can ask the client to apply an intensity measurement to it. You could ask, "On a scale of 0 to 10, how much of the red ball of anger do you feel in your stomach now?" The same applies to metaphors used with emotional issues. In the example of a broken heart, you could ask the client to look at the heart after several rounds and describe how it looks now, or how much of it is still broken.

Interestingly, there is a biological reason that metaphors, and imagery, work so well and can be such powerful tools in healing. The human brain has developed in a way that neural circuitry does not differentiate between the real and the symbolic. This phenomenon is called "neural confusion." According to Robert Sapolsky (2010), professor of biology, neurology, and neurosurgery at Stanford University, the brain treats literal images and metaphoric images as the same; this "neural confusion" gives symbols enormous power.

For example, if a person begins to eat a piece of food and realizes it is rotten, neurons in the area of the brain called the insula activate and cause a sensation of gustatory disgust. If you were to smell rotten food without tasting or eating it, the same neurons are activated and the same sensation is felt. Likewise, if you imagine eating something that you consider a disgusting food, the same neurons are activated and the same sensation is felt. Furthermore, and perhaps more significant, imagine you are watching the news and they are covering a story of a child predator and his latest victim. You might think, "What an awful person—that's so disgusting it makes me want to puke," triggering or activating the very same neurons in the insula. Similarly, you could recall something you once did and are ashamed of, and the brain reacts the same.

Sapolsky (2010) wrote, "When we evolved the capacity to be disgusted by moral failures, we didn't evolve a new brain region to handle it. Instead, the insula expanded its portfolio." There have been countless studies concerning the brain's inability to distinguish the literal from the symbolic or reality from metaphors and how these confused brain regions affect our daily activities and decisions.

This neural confusion was probably involved when we developed our interpretations of some of our experiences. We have convinced ourselves that our metaphoric interpretations are true. Sometimes we are completely convinced that we have much to be ashamed of and that we have massive limitations. The same mechanisms we used to develop "issues" can be used to loosen and dislodge our rigid and harmful beliefs.

Neural confusion is what allows metaphors to be so powerful in a therapeutic setting. It explains why they are effective in approaching and addressing myriad issues, from physical pain to emotional discomfort. This neural confusion allows us to use our cognitive flexibility and plasticity to resolve issues, so that, having resolved them, we are no longer confused regarding unreasonable versus reasonable ways to interpret what has happened to us, what we wish had happened to us, what we did to others that we want to take back, and what we never allowed ourselves to do previously because we thought we couldn't or shouldn't.

The Role of Intuition

A term that often appears in EFT and the helping fields is "intuition." There is much debate about what intuition is as well as where it comes from. One of the simplest exercises to demonstrate the existence of an intuitive response comes from EFT Master Rue Hass. In her workshops on EFT and intuition, she asks those in attendance to think of a decision they have to make, particularly one in which they feel conflict or find themselves over-analyzing. She asks attendees to imagine making the decision, one way or the other, and consider what that would be like, paying specific attention to what happens in the body. In one example, volunteer "Martha" imagined going to a conference that she was unsure about. When she imagined agreeing to attend, she described an "Oh no!' feeling and a tightening in her chest. This initial fear and body response is an intuitive response.

Each of us, at various times, has probably had an experience of feeling we should or should not do something. For instance, you get a "feeling" that you should not go down a particular street, or that you "should" call someone or that you "should" talk to a particular stranger in a room. Later, you find out there was a mugging or bad accident on that street; in calling your friend, you find she is in a crisis; and that stranger you addressed turns out to have just the information you need to finish a project you have been struggling with. These are basic examples of "intuition" at work. These examples have no root in the conscious, thinking mind. They are "gut reactions" that bypass cognitive processes. Intuition involves a "knowing" or surmising that is not based on clearly provided information, but that exists in the absence of immediately verifiable data.

The word "intuition" comes from the Latin *in-tuir*, or "looking, regarding, or knowing from within." Scholars have written about intuitive processes from the Aztec, Babylonian, Greek, Hebraic, and Chinese cultures (Franquemont, 1999). Pythagoras, Plato, and Aristotle discussed the topic. In the late 18th century, Immanuel Kant, "who believed that intuition was the non-rational recognition of an object" (Franquemont, 1999) set the stage for intuition rising to the foreground of 19th century philosophy, in which Henri Bergson suggested that while the intellect can analyze a person or event, complete knowledge can only be obtained through intuition. In the 20th century, psychiatrist Carl Jung suggested that intuition represents one of the significant ways in which human beings process the world around them. Later, he added that individuals might not only be unaware of how they know something, but also unaware of what they know.

Though there are historical ties between the work of Carl Jung and the concept of intuition, most scholars do not define the concept in Jungian psychoanalytic terms. There have been intense philosophical, scientific, psychological, and spiritual debates about what intuition is and how it works. Intuition is an abstract term. How you choose to define and apply it is up to you and your personal beliefs. In this book, we would like to touch on some of the definitions, research, and application of this abstract idea that you might find helpful and informative in EFT sessions.

As intuition is difficult to study objectively, much of the literature regarding intuition has focused on people's opinions rather than being data driven. It has also been difficult to develop a coherent theoretical framework, despite interest in the concept in the psychological sciences, education, management, and health industries. Although the literary sources provide differing, and at times conflicting, definitions of intuition, recent reviews of intuition literature and conceptual assessments of intuition as a scholarly term have included some comprehensive and generally agreed-upon definitions (Hodgkinson, Langan-Fox, & Sadler-Smith, 2008, p. 4). Vass (2012) defined intuition as "a complex set of inter-related cognitive, affective, and somatic processes in which there is no apparent intrusion of deliberate, rational thought." Dane and Pratt (2007, p. 40) defined intuitions as "affectively charged judgments that arise through rapid, non-conscious, and holistic associations."

Whether these definitions are interpreted in light of preexisting knowledge, a spiritual source, instinct, emotional knowing or sensitivity, electromagnetic fields of information as proposed in some interpretations of quantum mechanics theories, or something else is entirely up to the individual. Several authors have suggested, however, that this philosophical debate could be resolved if intuition were to be recognized as all of these things.

Some authors, including Frances Vaughan (1979), have proposed that intuition exists in levels or that there are "a variety of ways that human consciousness can access information without the use of a traditional analytic process" (Franquemont, 1999). Although there are several interpretations of even this singular approach, in his book *Awakening Intuition,* Vaughan (1979) describes four levels at which intuition might be accessed: physical, emotional, mental, and spiritual. We discuss these "levels of intuition" in this book because considering different levels of intuition provides a basic framework for understanding the various ways in which individuals approach and apply intuition. The concept of different levels suggests that some of the debate regarding the characteristics of intuition resulted from different people defining it differently and then arguing more about their definitions than the underlying phenomenon of intuition.

Physical Intuition

Physical intuition can be characterized by a strong bodily response. Perhaps while walking through the woods at night, you experience a drop in your stomach, increased heart rate, or shortness of breath. Perhaps you have experience goose bumps upon entering a room. These are examples of physical intuition, meaning that the body communicates or responds to information of which we are probably not consciously aware.

In *The Holistic Curriculum*, John P. Miller (2007) explains physical intuition by referencing a study by Charles Tart (1975), suggesting that it illustrates the mind-body connection. For example, the body usually gives the first clues that individuals are experiencing stress, even if they are not yet cognitively aware of it (Miller, p. 91). In his study, Charles Tart placed two subjects in two different soundproof rooms. In one, subject A was asked to press a button when he felt he had received a "subliminal stimulus" but was not given any direct stimulus. In the second soundproof room, subject B was receiving a low-level electric shock and was instructed to try to send a telepathic message to subject A with each shock so subject A would press the indicated button. "Interestingly, the key [button] taps were unrelated to the mental messages, but bodily responses were related to the mental messages" (Miller, p. 91).

In other words, brain-wave and heart-rate monitors placed on subject A indicated a heightened physical stress response in concert with the messages sent by subject B. The first person was responding to messages sent by the other, even though he was not aware of it except on a physical level. Note that, although Subject A's body responded to the indirect messages, Subject A did not consistently press the key in response to the indirect messages. Pressing the key is a conscious decision. Bodily responses are energetic or subconscious reactions. Sometimes our conscious decisions inaccurately represent our energetic or subconscious reactions.

David Feinstein, PhD, writes about the information that is carried by energy. In the countless wireless devices we use today, including cellphones and Wi-Fi devices, electromagnetic waves, radio waves, and other forms of invisible energy can carry information over thousands of miles. The same is thought to be true of our energy systems. Just as the previous carry your phone calls and e-mails to colleagues and loved ones, a person's energy field carries psychological information and memory (Feinstein, 2013, p. 81). This information can be sensed, picked up, and at times, felt by others. Many energy practitioners consider themselves particularly sensitive to the information held in others' energy fields.

Sometimes our bodies are more sensitive to the emotions, stressors, and energy shifts our clients experience throughout EFT sessions. Humans appear to be extremely attuned to the subtle reactions of others, perhaps evolving from our need to perceive danger. You might see a subtle physical change or response in your client and you may also have a reaction to your clients' responses; sometimes a "gut feeling" is literally a feeling in your gut. Not only can this physical intuition provide you with direction or information regarding your clients, but it can also be beneficial to remember that sometimes clients' cognitive processes might need to catch up with the clues and information that their physical body is indicating.

Practitioners often see the effects of an energy shift on the client's face before the client actually recognizes that a shift has happened. Other physical clues can indicate, not only whether shifts have occurred, but also whether intensities are rising or falling. For example, pay attention to posture, facial color or expression, breathing, yawning, shaking, twitching, and so on. While discussing a particular event, clients might communicate to you that their intensity has lessened, but physical clues, such as a suddenly rigid posture, sweating, or an increased breathing rate, might signal that there is another aspect that needs to be addressed, or that the client has moved on to a different event or memory altogether.

Both the signals you note from the client's physiology and your own internal reactions are a source of valuable information throughout sessions. As always, check in often with your client to test the accuracy and applicability of the information you gather.

Emotional Intuition

Emotional intuition refers to the experience of intuition through feelings. Have you ever walked into a room and, despite the absence of any overt physical clues, known that the people in the room had just been arguing? Or perhaps you've sat down next to someone and immediately sensed that person's sadness, even though nothing that person said or did could have given it away. Have you noticed yourself "sizing up" people upon meeting them, based solely on the feelings you get from them or from being around them, without any experiences or concrete information from which to draw? These are examples of what Vaughan classifies as emotional intuition.

"Humans are able to perceive emotional information before engaging in rational thought" (Myers, 2002, p. 1). Cognitive science has found that, biologically, there is ancient and necessary wisdom in our ability to make split-second decisions about the nature of people we encounter. This emotional intuition is created or supported by pathways that run from the eye to the brain's emotional control centers (i.e., the limbic system), completely bypassing the cortex, allowing us to process information in milliseconds, outside of conscious thought. Once the cortex interprets the information, however, the thinking brain takes over. Evolutionarily, when meeting a fellow caveman or stranger in the woods while hunting, the one with the ability to quickly and accurately decide "friend or foe?" would be more likely to survive and leave descendants. This "helps explain why humans today can distinguish at a glance between facial expressions of anger, sadness, fear, or pleasure" (Myers, 2002, p. 1).

Harvard psychology professors Nalini Ambady, PhD, and Robert Rosenthal, PhD, studied how accurately people made these split-second, unconscious emotional intuitions regarding sizing up other people (Ambady & Rosenthal, 1992). The professors videotaped several of their colleagues and showed observers 10-second clips from the beginning, middle, and end of a class. The observers were then asked to rate the instructors' confidence, energy, and warmth. "They found that these ratings predicted with amazing accuracy the average student rating taken at semester's end" (Myers, 2002, p. 1). Interestingly, even smaller clips of only two seconds yielded similarly accurate results.

New York University professor and psychologist John Bargh, PhD, repeated similar studies (Bargh, Chen, & Burrows, 1996) and found that students respond to images flashed for just two-tenths of a second. He commented, "We're finding that everything is evaluated as good or bad within a quarter of a second. So before engaging in rational thought, we may find ourselves either loathing or loving a piece of art or our new neighbor" (Myers, 2002, p. 1).

Similarly, there have been several studies on the role of the heart in the intuitive process. A 2004 study (McCraty, Atkinson, & Bradley) demonstrated electrophysiological evidence of intuitive feeling, as well as surprising results involving the heart. We already know that the brain can process information while bypassing the cerebral cortex and conscious thought, but this study found that the heart contributes to this process. Study participants were shown a randomized series of emotionally triggering images, both positive and negative, while researchers recorded a variety of physical signals, including baseline temperature, skin conductance, and heart rate. Researchers observed that the heart accurately received and responded to intuitive information. That is, changes in heart rate based on future stimuli were the first indicators of response in nearly all participants. Put simply, before being shown a negative image, most participants' heart rates increased significantly, and preceding a positive image, heart rates slowed. This occurred even though they were unaware of whether the next image would be positive or negative. Researchers were also able to demonstrate data showing that this pre-stimulus information is communicated to the brain.

When it comes to EFT, emotional intuition can play a significant role in how you read and approach your client. Pay attention to the feelings you have throughout a session. You may find yourself with a sense of how your clients are feeling, even if they are not able to verbalize it at the moment, just as when you walk into a room and know two people have been arguing. At times, clients can be so close to their own story, or so desensitized to the emotional weight of the information they're sharing, that they are unaware of what they are experiencing emotionally. In contrast, you might discover that you are able to pick up the true state of their emotions. Even a split second of a facial expression can communicate a great deal of information.

When teaching intuition, Karin reminds her students that all the information one intuitively senses must then be passed through the client's filter. In other words, you may have a strong feeling of sadness from your client, but it is not generally advisable for you to say, "You're sad" and move forward, no matter how sure you are. If you have developed the rapport to support it, consider a question such as "Is there sadness or something similar here?" It is important to ask it in a questioning tone (rather than more of a statement) and/or facial expression, and wait for their response. Or ask if clients are feeling something in the category of sadness or unhappiness, inviting clients to interpret your comments or questions and provide for you the words that are right for them. What you sensed as "sadness" might be described by your client as "forlorn" or "devastated." Those feelings might seem the same as sad to you, but it is your client's emotional experience and language that will continue to guide the session in the right direction.

Use the information you gather through intuition to gather even more information. By offering possibilities and asking questions, you allow clients to define the specifics of the emotions or sensations you felt.

Mental Intuition

According to Vaughan, intuition is often experienced on a mental level in the form of images or flashes of insight. This can be described in two ways. First, many researchers have cited intuition as access to knowledge that is not part of one's normal consciousness in which the end products of implicit learning experiences are stored below the level of conscious awareness (Reber, 1993; Dienes & Berry, 1997). In other words, prior learning, experiences, and expertise can be stored outside of the conscious mind and "appear" without conscious thought. For example, individuals may intuitively know how to complete a task even though they have no conscious prior experience or knowledge regarding how to do so.

In the early 1990s, neuroscientists made an important discovery about empathy and passive learning, called "mirror neurons" (Winerman, 2005, p. 48). Mirror neurons are brain cells that respond the same when one performs an action or observes someone else doing the same thing. According to Giacomo Rizzolatti, MD, among the researchers at the University of Parma who discovered mirror neurons, "the neurons could help explain how and why we 'read' other people's minds and feel empathy for them" (Winerman, 2005, p. 48). The concept is still in its infancy but is considered a major step in understanding mental intuition and base human concepts such as empathy and language development.

Similarly, Vaughan (1979), Miller (2007), Franquemont (1999), and others have classified the "aha!" experience of mental insight, innovation, genius, and artistry as a form of mental intuition. This is sometimes referred to as "creative intuition." Miller describes this as insight "permeated with intense energy and passion, that brings about great clarity" (2007, p. 93).

Regardless of which classification of mental intuition one adopts, the basis of the term lies in insight that originates outside of conscious, rational thought. Most psychologists and researchers agree on at least one of several dual-process theories of cognition. Put simply, "thinking, memory, and attitude operate on two levels: the conscious/deliberate and the unconscious/automatic" (Myers, 2002, p. 1). This is called dual processing.

As authors write, they are engaging in a dual mental process. For example, while reading shorthand notes, authors' cognitive processes continue to assemble and form sentences, pulling details from information they have read previously, while the authors' fingers type under the guidance and instruction of... *somewhere*. Authors are not consciously thinking about how the keyboard works, where their fingers are landing as they type, and their brains are usually forming the next two sentences before completing the one they're physically typing. This is dual mental processing. In the same way, that *somewhere* can offer up flashes of insight, information, and clarity, seemingly completely apart from the conscious mind. There is certainly some debate as to where this unconscious information originates, but it does not appear to come from conscious, rational cognition.

As an EFT practitioner, you might experience flashes of insight and clarity throughout your sessions. You subconscious mind is functioning in many ways at once. Part of it is functioning holographically, creating multidimensional perceptions based on available data. Part of it is functioning more specifically, drawing parallels and sifting through information of which you are consciously unaware.

Nonetheless, even though these insights can be very helpful, some practitioners might doubt these spontaneous bits of information too much to feel comfortable sharing them. We encourage you to share your spontaneous intuitive insights in a respectful way, then check in with the client to see how timely, accurate, or appropriate your intuitions are for a particular person.

For example, while in sessions, it sometimes occurs to Kari Tumminia to use tools or approaches from previous sessions, even when she might not realize she remembered them. In considering whether to use a particular tool, approach, or phrase, no matter what it is, she remains sensitive to her clients and what is going on for them at that moment. If the timing seems right, and she has enough rapport, she may make a suggestion and see how it lands, ask to try a new approach, or ask how a particular phrase or word fits for the client.

Practitioners need always to remain open to being wrong. If clients say, or merely indicate, that you're wrong, listen closely. They will often provide more information as they explain how you're wrong. If they say that you're right, they will often provide more information as they explain how you're right. Everything is an opportunity to gather more information; when you are listening with an open mind, your clients will ultimately provide you with all the information you need to help them get what they need.

Spiritual Intuition

Vaughan describes spiritual intuition as being "independent from feelings, thoughts, and sensations" (Vaughan, 1979, p. 77). We will define spiritual intuition as information that occurs from outside human input. For some, this kind of intuition may come from a deity or spiritual figure; for example, many Christians believe that intuition—or, in this case, inner knowing—comes from the anointing of the Holy Spirit (1 John 2). Still others believe that all of humanity is interconnected. Mahayana Buddhism embraces a teaching called *shunyata,* which posits the idea that humans are not separate, autonomous beings; rather, we are all one. Some interpret this to mean that intuitive insight is available to us through our connectedness.

In the same way, and perhaps offering an additional interpretation of spiritual intuition, some interpretations of recent research in quantum physics suggest that all of our experiences are made up of electromagnetic fields. From this perspective, the only reason physical objects, including ourselves, exist is because particles behave differently under observation (as in Feynman's double-slit experiment in 1965). Quantum mechanics discoveries are sometimes interpreted to mean that all information is accessible in fields, which ties into the idea of "collective consciousness," sometimes referred to as "field consciousness" or "unified field consciousness."

Collective consciousness is "a mode of awareness that emerges at the first transpersonal stage of consciousness, when our identities expand beyond our egos. A crucial capacity that accompanies this awareness is the ability to intuitively sense and work with the interactions between our and others' energy fields, physically, emotionally, mentally and spiritually" (Kenny, 2004, p. 1). Many researchers now speculate that energy fields, or regions of influence, explain the phenomenon of collective consciousness.

The concept of fields of influence is not new, or unfounded. Electric, magnetic, and gravitational fields are forces of influence that are invisible without special equipment and are considered scientific fact. Similarly, the concept of morphogenetic fields, underlying the form of a growing organism (Kenny, 2004, p. 10), is generally accepted by most biologists, even though they are unable to explain how those fields developed or exactly how they work.

Biochemist and physiologist Rupert Sheldrake postulated in 1999 that morphogenetic fields are actually part of a larger category of fields called morphic fields (Kenny, 2004, p. 10), that connect us to what we experience. These morphic fields organize and coordinate behavior in social groups and across distances. He further suggests that morphic resonance might enable us to perceive each other's images, thoughts, impressions, or feelings, even if we are thousands of miles apart. Such a phenomenon might be similar to, if not identical with telepathy (Kenny, 2004, p. 10).

Sheldrake and his colleagues have conducted a number of experiments on humans and animals that seem to support his hypothesis. The simplest of these involved using synchronized video cameras in dog owners' workplaces and homes. Sheldrake and his team observed that dogs consistently went to the door to wait as soon as their owners decided to return home from work, even when the times varied on a daily basis.

Similarly, Sheldrake and others have demonstrated that learning can occur across distances, even among humans. In a number of studies, one group of people was asked to solve a particular puzzle. After they had solved it, the same puzzle was then broadcast to a new group of people across the world. People in the new group, who had not seen the puzzle before, were able to solve it faster than the original group of people had solved it. A third group completed it still faster, apparently benefiting from the problem-solving work of people who had gone before them (Kenny, 2004, p. 1).

This only serves as a very brief introduction to a very complex subject, on which there is new research emerging daily. This type of scientific advancement can help us further understand intuition and how it operates on a level outside of human perception. That is not to say that science trumps spirituality. Rather, this is to suggest that human beings, energy, and intuition are so wonderfully complex that our most brilliant minds have only begin to scratch the surface of how they work. Whether you choose to believe in spiritual intuition as interconnectedness, God, angels, the Universe, biology, quantum mechanics, or something entirely different, remember that in EFT, the client is the focus. This means that we need to be sensitive to the client's spiritual context, whatever that may be.

We benefit from checking with clients whether their spiritual approach, beliefs, and attitudes are similar or different from our own. If practitioners and clients appear to have similar spiritual ideas and practices, practitioners might assume agreement in all areas, which would not necessarily be accurate. If practitioners and clients appear to have different spiritual ideas and practices, practitioners might assume they differ in all areas, which would also not necessarily be accurate. At other times, a client might find particular wording or the suggestion of certain spiritual approaches or contexts offensive. Making assumptions about clients' spiritual context, whether the same or different from yours, can deeply damage rapport or bring about unnecessary difficulties in a session.

Many practitioners, including the authors of this book, ask for basic spiritual and religious information during the intake process. Include questions such as: How would you define your religious or spiritual beliefs? Do you believe we have one life or many lives? Do you believe in hell? These questions help clarify your clients' perspectives and help you adapt your language and approach in ways that enhance rapport and that invite clients to express their beliefs and opinions freely. If, for any reason, clients were to react negatively or defensively to your questions, it would be valuable to ascertain what just happened, explaining clearly that your intent was not to be offensive or off-putting in any way. Sometimes it works well to ask clients how you might better gain that background information from them. By including clients in your problem-solving strategies regarding how best to ask them questions, you are likely to increase rapport and facilitate the progress of sessions.

Intuition is best used when practitioners are able to get out of their own way. This includes being open to receiving and recognizing intuitive information, as well as utilizing it during sessions in a way that maintains focus on the client. As you gather information with your eyes and ears, you gain information from however your clients respond, which often might not be the way you expect them to, prefer them to, or wish they did.

There is no right or wrong when it comes to intuition. This does not mean that you can never be wrong regarding your intuitions. We definitely make mistakes with our typical five senses, but we still basically rely on them. For example, you might look at a tiny piece of lint on the floor and believe it's a bug. You might mishear the words someone stated, but you still generally rely on your hearing. Similarly, you might misinterpret an intuitive hypothesis, but you could still utilize that guess to address an issue in a new way with clients. The more calm and accepting you are regarding intuition, yours and your clients, the more effectively you are likely to develop the skill of gathering information through intuition. The more intensely you intentionally try to be intuitive, the more likely you are to interfere with your ability to gather intuitive ideas.

As an abstract term, intuition is defined, interpreted, and applied to the human experience in many different ways. This description of intuition and several of its facets is not intended to be a complete resource but to raise questions that you might want to pursue in your work on yourself as well as with clients.

Developing Your Intuition

Though there are many definitions and theories of intuition, most agree that intuition is something that happens quickly without rational and conscious thought.

Many practitioners find that the more experience they have with energy approaches the greater their ability to "hear," trust, and utilize their intuitive skills. Developing this skill is not to be hurried along but is to be enjoyed and appreciated. How can one encourage the development of intuition? When it comes to EFT, the best advice is:

- **Get out of your own way.** The term "get out of your own way" has been used so often throughout the EFT world that it has nearly become meaningless; many of us may read it or hear it without ever thinking about how it actually applies. To the authors, getting out of your own way means becoming aware that your personal perspective has the ability to affect everything that happens in the context of an EFT session, including your intuition. The more you are aware of your own issues, triggers, filters, opinions, attitudes, and perceptions, the more you can very intentionally move them to the side (or, in some cases, resolve them altogether) so that they don't interfere with your work as an EFT practitioner. Getting out of your own way is an *ongoing* process of self-awareness, self-evaluation, doing your own work. It develops your ability to be fully present in the moment. This increase of self-awareness is a process that does not end—each of us will always have "stuff" to deal with—but the process is well worth it, and vital for a truly successful EFT practice.

- **The focus is always on the client first.** Offer gentle options to test information or feelings and gather specifics through the client's filter.

- **Be sensitive to your client's level of openness and spiritual context.**

- **EFT will work with or without grand intuitive insights.** Intuition is helpful but is not a requirement for using EFT effectively.

Advanced Pain and Serious Disease

In the *EFT Level 2 Comprehensive Training Resource,* you read in Chapter 9 about physical issues and how EFT can be used to address them. Pain has an emotional component, and the experience of pain can often be reduced or even eliminated when the emotional aspects are addressed. To help further your understanding, we will explore some additional concepts for using EFT with pain as well as with serious disease.

Let's begin by pointing out again that none of the information offered in this book is intended as a substitute for medical advice, to diagnose, or to treat anyone. We strongly recommend that you consult your health professional for medical advice and treatment regarding your own medical or physical concerns and that you recommend that your clients consult their own health professionals if they have symptoms about which they are concerned. EFT is intended as a complementary practice. It does not "treat" or "cure" any medical issue. As always, practice EFT and any other modality within the realm of your professional qualifications. Adhere to the rules, regulations, and guidelines of your profession or licensing body.

The Mind-Body Connection

You have read about and may have personal experience with the emotional aspects of physical pain and illness. In Level 2, you were introduced to the concept of stress aggravating pain and how long-term exposure to stress can impact existing conditions, possibly leading to serious health problems. This is an example of what is often termed the "mind-body connection," a concept derived from the biopsychosocial (BPS) model theorized by psychiatrist George Engel (1980). The BPS model, or mind-body connection, is the interaction of the physical, mental, emotional, and social aspects of the human life experience. It illustrates a connection between the state of one's mind and emotions and the state of one's body.

Philosophically, the distinction between the mind and the body as two different entities can be traced to the Greeks. Both Plato and Aristotle distinguished between the mind and the body in their early writing. French mathematician, philosopher, and physiologist Rene Descartes "gave the first systematic account for the mind-body relationship" (Blutner, n.d.), claiming that the mind and the brain are different substances. In other words, the brain, as part of the body, was physical, while the mind was not. This dualism of substances is now known as Cartesian dualism, and maintains that while the mind and body are different substances, they are intimately related and can affect one another.

In the early 1880s, while working with a patient he called Anna O, Joseph Breuer substantiated Descartes' claim that the mind affects the body (Launer, 2005, p. 465). Anna O fell ill in 1880 at the age of 21 and sought treatment from Dr. Breuer, a distinguished physician and eminent neurophysiologist. According to Dr. Breuer, Anna O had been healthy up until that point in her life, and had shown no previous signs of neurosis or physical illness. He described her as being markedly intelligent and "under control of a sharp and critical common sense" (Launer, 2005, p. 466). Despite her previous good health, Anna O was experiencing partial paralysis of three of her four limbs, weakness, inability to turn her head, nervous cough, loss of appetite, hallucinations, agitation, mood swings, abusive and destructive behavior, amnesia, tunnel vision, and speech problems; according to Breuer's reports, Anna ceased to conjugate verbs, and eventually only used infinitives (Launer, 2005, p. 466).

In 1881 and 1882, Breuer and Anna O spent nearly 1,000 hours in sessions. Noting that the onset of Anna's symptoms correlated directly with the sudden illness and death of her father the year before, Breuer claimed that by spending time recalling and talking about her emotional and intense experiences during the last months of her father's life, Anna was able to make connections between the individual experiences of the traumatic time and her individual symptoms. Dr. Breuer reported that, as Anna identified the triggers of each of her symptoms and talked through them "in vivid emotion," the relevant symptoms would disappear (Launer, 2005, p. 466).

Since its publication, Breuer's account of Anna O has given rise to a tremendous amount of debate. Although it has been heavily criticized, it is significant because it represents one of the first times that the mind-body connection—the idea that Anna's emotional state could cause her physical symptoms—was both recognized and applied in diagnosis and treatment.

Kathryn Sherrod, PhD, a therapist in private practice in Nashville, Tennessee, has over 40 years of experience in the field of psychology. Since receiving her doctorate in 1972, she has published research, taught graduate and undergraduate courses, worked at a state psychiatric hospital for children and youth, and run her own practice. More recently, she has studied energy modalities with both Ann and Karin, and graciously agreed to share an article on the history of the mind-body connection.

Science and the Mind-Body Connection

By Kathryn Sherrod, PhD

The relationship between emotions and the body has been considered important since the beginning of modern medicine. Claude Bernard, a French physiologist, developed the concept of the milieu interieur (or the environment inside) in the mid-1800s. In 1865, Bernard wrote that our bodies support us by consistently regulating warmth (or cooling), hydration, and other necessary conditions for life. He believed that illness and death represent an interference or perturbation of those mechanisms (Bernard, 1957; Cohen, 1957).

In 1932, Walter Cannon, a professor of physiology at Harvard University coined the now commonly used term "homeostasis, from the Greek homo-ios, meaning "similar," and *stasis,* meaning "position." Homeostasis refers to how our bodies make efforts to return to a stable state. When working with animals, Cannon noticed that changes in animals' emotional state, such as anxiety, distress, or rage, was accompanied by cessation of stomach movements so the animals could not adequately digest their food (Cannon, 1929). These studies into the relationship between the effects of emotions and perceptions on the autonomic nervous system (namely, the sympathetic and parasympathetic responses) initiated the recognition of the fight, flight, or freeze response.

Psychoneuroimmunology (PNI) is the study of the interaction between psychological processes and the nervous and immune systems of the human body (Ader, Felten, & Cohen, 2007). PNI uses a multidisciplinary approach, including data from the fields of psychology, neuroscience, immunology, physiology, genetics, pharmacology, molecular biology, psychiatry, behavioral medicine, infectious diseases, endocrinology, and rheumatology. The main interests of PNI are the interactions between the nervous and immune systems plus the relationships between mental processes and health. This all began in 1975 when psychologist Robert Ader and immunologist Nicholas Cohen, who were at the University of Rochester, demonstrated PNI with classical conditioning of an immune function, from which they coined the term "psychoneuroimmunology."

Ader was investigating how long laboratory rats might remember conditioned responses (in the way that Pavlov conditioned dogs to drool when they heard a bell ring). To condition the rats, he used saccharin-flavored water (the conditioned stimulus) and the drug Cytoxan, which unconditionally induces nausea, taste aversion, and suppression of the immune system. Ader was surprised to discover that after conditioning, just feeding the rats saccharin-laced water was associated with the death of some animals. He hypothesized that they had been immunosuppressed after receiving the conditioned stimulus.

Ader and Cohen tested this hypothesis directly by deliberately immunizing conditioned and unconditioned animals, exposing these and other control groups to the conditioned taste stimulus, and then measuring the amount of antibody produced. The results were reproducible and revealed that conditioned rats exposed to the conditioned stimulus indeed had suppressed immune systems. In other words, a signal via the nervous system (taste) was affecting immune function. This was one of the first scientific experiments that demonstrated that the nervous system can affect the immune system.

In 1981, David Felten, then at the Indiana University School of Medicine, discovered a network of nerves leading to blood vessels as well as to cells of the immune system. The researchers also found nerves in the thymus gland (part of the immune system) and the spleen (which is related to people's ability to handle stress) terminating near clusters of immune system cells (i.e., lymphocytes, macrophages, and mast cells). This discovery provided one of the first indications of how neuro-immune interaction occurs. In 1981, Ader, Cohen, and Felten edited the groundbreaking book *Psychoneuroimmunology*, which laid out the underlying premise that the brain and immune system represent a single, integrated system of defense.

In 1985, research by neuropharmacologist Candace Pert, funded by the National Institutes of Health, revealed that neuropeptide-specific receptors are present on the cell walls in the brain and the immune system. The discovery by Pert and her colleagues that neuropeptides and neurotransmitters act directly on the immune system shows their close association with emotions and suggests mechanisms through which emotions and immunology are interdependent. Showing that the immune and endocrine systems are modulated by the entire central nervous system has improved our understanding of emotions, as well as of disease. *Molecules of Emotion,* Pert's 1999 book on underlying aspects of emotions, is both informative and fascinating to read.

Further Research

Today, there have been significant advances in medical, psychological, and other scientific research that support the existence of the mind-body connection. Researchers studying the placebo effect (the beneficial effect after treatment that results from the subject's expectations rather than from the treatment itself) at the

University of Michigan have provided what they call "concrete evidence" of the mind-body connection (Archer, 2006). Their research shows that, though many have dismissed the placebo effect as an imagined or purely psychological phenomenon, the placebo effect actually involves changes in brain chemistry that affect pain receptors in the brain, resulting in a reduction of pain that is explained by an underlying physiological effect.

In the study, researchers caused pain in healthy, male volunteers by injecting seawater solution into their jaw muscles, scanning their brains to observe the pain response. During a second scan, researchers repeated the procedure, this time telling participants that they would receive a medication, which was, in fact, a placebo, that could relieve their pain. One hundred percent of participants showed an increase in activation of the body's natural pain relief response in reaction to the promised medication that would reduce pain. In over half the subjects, pain signals in the brain dropped by more than 20%.

The researchers conducting this study pointed out that this could help explain why people experience relief from noninvasive techniques and/or remedies that do not involve physical or chemical intervention. Similar studies have demonstrated that practices such as meditation reduce brain activity in the primary somatosensory cortex, which is the part of the brain that creates the feeling of where and how intensely the physical sensation of pain is felt. This research illustrates the reality of the mind-body connection and provides the beginning of an understanding of the power of noninvasive techniques such as EFT.

If, however, someone were to suggest that EFT creates "placebo" effects rather than "real effects," it would be apparent that this individual does not yet comprehend what a placebo effect is. A placebo effect occurs when someone strongly believes that something benign, such as a glass of water or a sugar pill, will have a specific effect on the body. Believing that this effect will occur, people then actually create the expected effects using their own brains, bodies, and energy systems. That is, there are measurable physiological effects in response to taking substances that cannot possibly have a major physiological effect. Glasses of water and tiny sugar pills do not generally result in demonstrable physiological changes, but believing that an effect will occur does allow people to create measurable physiological changes.

In addition to people experiencing positive effects from benign or neutral substances, people can also experience negative effects from benign or neutral substances. This reaction, which is the opposite of the placebo effect, is called the "nocebo effect." Originally, the term was used in pharmacology research and was restricted to meaning that someone had a harmful, injurious, unpleasant, or undesirable reaction to something that could not logically have caused a negative reaction (e.g., more water and sugar pills). These reactions were actually self-created by people who had a pessimistic belief or expectation that the benign substance would produce harmful, injurious, unpleasant, or undesirable consequences. It is important to remember that, despite the fact that there is no "real" drug involved, the actual harmful, injurious, unpleasant, or undesirable biochemical, physiological, behavioral, emotional, and/or cognitive consequences of the administration of the inert drug are very real.

Stress and Emotion

We have the power in our bodies and in our energy systems to create massive changes in us. Some of those changes are beneficial and some are not so beneficial. For example, carrying around old anger is associated with wear and tear on many aspects of bodily functioning. EFT harnesses our energetic system's power in positive ways that can help people give their bodies what they need to heal from both emotional and physical pain. Using old stored-up anger as an example, many people discover that they feel better when they release pent-up anger that they have clung to for decades, almost as if it were a security blanket providing emotional support instead of being an anchor that is holding them down.

Researchers at the University of California–Los Angeles have found that stress-related hormones such as cortisol suppress enzymes within immune cells, making the individual significantly more susceptible to illness and disease. Each cell in our bodies contains a protective cap called a telomere, which can be compared to a tiny clock that shortens in length every time the cell divides. Short telomeres have been linked to a range of human diseases, including HIV, heart disease, osteoporosis, and Alzheimer's, among others. Fortunately, each cell also contains an enzyme called telomerase that helps to keep cells young by preserving the length of the cell's telomere and ensuring its ability to continue dividing. The researchers at UCLA found that the stress hormone cortisol "suppresses immune cells' ability to activate their telomerase" (University of California–Los Angeles, 2008), explaining why people under chronic stress have shorter telomeres in their cells and, therefore, high occurrences of serious disease.

Furthermore, Gregory Miller, PhD, discovered that in people who experience significant life stressors, such as caregivers who are responsible for family members with illnesses, the pattern of gene expression in white blood cells involved in the body's immune response was altered so that it was less responsive to hormones that should tell the body to shut down the fight-or-flight response triggered by stress (Elsevier, 2008).

These studies, along with many others, contribute to an ever-growing body of evidence for the mind-body connection, showing that physical illness and disease are more reasonably treated holistically than only with physical interventions or medications.

The concept of the mind-body connection and its increasing acceptance are very important to our work with EFT and pain, physical symptoms, and serious disease. EFT allows us to address factors of physical pain and serious disease that are not always addressed by conventional medicine approaches.

We would like to take a moment here to reiterate that this book is not intended to criticize or take away from conventional medical practices. We believe in a holistic approach to disease and physical issues, and this includes physical and medical intervention, when necessary. Again, always encourage your clients to seek professional medical advice if they are experiencing pain or have a physical issue. The ideal environment for healing is represented by a partnership among different approaches, including EFT and professional medical assistance.

However, once we accept the assumption that the mind and body are, in fact, connected and can affect one another in significant ways, using EFT to address issues of pain and serious disease becomes a logical solution. Practitioners and clients all over the world are reporting significant success rates when using EFT as part of a holistic approach to disease and pain. Again, we are not saying to avoid allopathic medicine (i.e., approaches conventional physicians would utilize). Instead, we are suggesting that EFT and other alternative approaches can be used in conjunction with standard Western medicine.

Addressing Physical Issues with EFT

People are often surprised to learn that there is no "special" version of EFT for dealing with serious diseases or physical issues and pain. EFT practitioners approach serious diseases and pain the same way that we would approach any other issue, by: following the lead of the client, finding core issues, addressing specific emotions/events/physical symptoms that may affect the core issues, addressing all of the aspects of each issue, testing, and being persistent.

Although physical issues may seem more complex or serious than many emotional issues, part of the challenge for practitioners lies in their perception of physical issues. Practitioners may find themselves overwhelmed at the thought of working with chronic or terminal illnesses. With persistence, consistency, and a solid understanding of the basic EFT skill set, however, EFT and you as a practitioner can play a significant role in the holistic approach to serious disease.

It helps to realize that both physical problems and emotional issues are all energy, so to speak. That is, sometimes before issues become entrenched enough to affect a person emotionally or physically, those issues can be detected in the individual's energy system. EFT is one of the energy treatments that can address issues at all levels: energetic, physical, and emotional. After all, they are all connected to each other. No one issue is isolated from the others.

If you approach serious disease as an overarching issue to which unresolved occurrences in the individual's life contribute, you can use your basic EFT skills and understanding of specific events, core issues, and aspects to help your client methodically bring up and collapse the emotional factors contributing to his or her physical state. As you approach the overarching issue of a serious disease or physical issue, there are several approaches that can be useful in breaking it into more manageable pieces.

Symptoms

Helping your client experience symptomatic relief can be a good place to start. Often, the immediate experience of symptoms can be decreased, which can encourage clients to continue working through other aspects of their physical issue with EFT. Be aware, however, that resolution of serious diseases and physical issues is rarely reached by focusing on symptoms alone.

Specific Events

Most often, addressing issues of serious disease will revolve around finding and working with relevant specific events. A practitioner focuses on helping clients find specific events that could be related to the physical issue and/or serious disease. This often takes some detective work, with questions such as "What was going on in your life at, or just before, the time of diagnosis?" or "When can you remember first feeling this way?" or "What is your theory as to the cause of this?" or "If there were an emotional component to this, what would it be?" Sometimes you can prompt clients to help with this investigative process by asking, "If you were me, what questions would you be asking?" or "Have you wondered in the back of your mind if this might be related to something else?"

Pain as a Message

When using EFT as part of a holistic approach to addressing serious disease and pain, it can be beneficial to work with your clients toward accepting the physical ailment as a legitimate part of them rather than trying to reject it or get rid of it. Perhaps this could involve looking at the physical issue as a part of their body that is currently "using an inappropriate method of communicating something positive to us, [such as] the misunderstood teenager who goes on a destructive spree in order to command attention" (Roberts, n.d.). This shift in perspective can serve as an effective metaphor for clients seeking specific information on which to tap, for example, asking, "If this physical issue were your body trying to communicate with you, what would it be saying?" If asking clients what their body is trying to communicate to them does not seem to prompt them toward increased clarity or specificity, you can ask what they might want to tell their bodies, their illness, or their pain.

The Personal Peace Procedure

Most clients will benefit by continuing to address their issues on their own. Some practitioners recommend that people who are working on serious disease issues tap every day, when possible. One of the easier ways to encourage your client to tap between sessions, preferably daily, is to help them develop their own Personal Peace Procedure (see *EFT Level 1 Comprehensive Training Resource* or the tutorial at EFTUniverse.com). The Personal Peace Procedure can provide clients with a framework to work through memories, trauma, emotions, and issues on their own and between sessions, which can often shorten the healing process.

For some people, creating a list of *all* their issues is a daunting and overwhelming task, especially when dealing with a serious medical issue. Help clients create their lists and break the items down into small specific "chunks." Ann once had a client who became emotionally upset at the mere thought of making a lengthy list. Perhaps you could help them pick one or two less intense events to begin working with on their own, or simply start by focusing on how well they are breathing in the moment. Make sure they understand how to get and stay specific and to identify aspects of one issue at a time. Encourage them to begin with smaller issues. Teach them what to do if they become upset. Encourage them to bring the list with them to their EFT session and make discussing progress an important part of the session.

If working on a list of events is too overwhelming for them, help them create a shorter, more manageable list and encourage them to develop a plan for tapping for short periods several times a day on whatever they are feeling at the time. Although the Personal Peace Procedure sounds simple in explanation—make a list of events and address each one, one at a time—it can be a daunting task in practice. Help them make it manageable in their daily lives. Help them picture their daily activities and when would be a good time to add tapping into their existing routines.

Address the Diagnosis

The experience of learning that you have a serious disease or chronic illness can be almost as traumatizing as having the disease itself. Some clients report that the way they were told about their diagnosis seemed callous or shocking. Discover and address each aspect of the memory of receiving the diagnosis, such as tone of voice, shock, and perceived support (or lack thereof) from medical staff, friends, family, colleagues, and others. Some clients may need help processing the reality and nature of their diagnosis. For instance, a person diagnosed with cancer might have myriad negative emotions that stem from just the word or idea of "cancer." Help your clients clarify the feelings and thoughts they have about the diagnosis.

Treatment

Again, EFT is not a tool to "cure" serious diseases and physical ailments. Emma Roberts, an EFT Master and cofounder of the EFT Centre in London, has worked extensively with cancer patients using EFT. She writes, "EFT does not claim to offer a cure for cancer, but is a powerful support for positive wellbeing. It provides an immediate tool for managing this ongoing emotional rollercoaster, helping to calm and rebalance the energy system whilst it adjusts to what is happening. From the start, EFT can be used to help clear the blocks to healing, both physical and emotional" (Roberts, n.d.).

Utilize EFT as a complement to any treatment protocol or procedure the individual is currently undergoing. Emma states that EFT often reduces the impact of the side effects of cancer treatments. Addressing side effects from treatment, both physical and emotional, as well as worries, nerves, feelings of lack of control, and other concerns provides a way for clients to resolve stuck energy around these issues. EFT is a wonderful tool for clients to feel empowered, as they have an avenue to participate actively in their treatment.

An Individual Journey

While working through the process of addressing serious disease and pain with clients, you will likely utilize the full content of your EFT toolbox, which includes a variety of techniques and approaches. Remember that each person's experience with physical ailments and disease is a personal, individual journey. People react differently to their circumstances and experiences. You might discover that some people do not want to use EFT for their physical issues. Sometimes, people who begin using EFT as a complement to their medical treatment choose to stop. As practitioners, we respect the experience and decisions of our individual clients, remembering, as always, that everything we need for successful EFT sessions comes from our clients. This is true with serious diseases, as well as with other issues.

EFT practitioner and trainer Alina Frank specializes in using EFT for sex and intimacy challenges. She shared with us a case study concerning a woman with a chronic condition known as vulvar vestibulitis syndrome (VVS). It serves as a helpful example of how to approach a chronic or serious physical ailment. In this case, Alina describes how to deal with a problem that resulted from a collection of stresses or challenges to equanimity. Sometimes there is not a single large, obvious trauma attached to a chronic condition.

Case Study: Chronic Vulvar Vestibulitis Syndrome
By Alina Frank

Samantha came because she had been dealing for about 10 years with a condition known as vulvar vestibulitis syndrome (VVS). By the time she started working with me, she had tried everything: topical over-the-counter and prescription treatments of all varieties, acupuncture, supplements, as well as seeing several doctors. VVS is known to cause severe, sometimes debilitating vaginal pain that can range from mild irritation to a burning or cutting sensation that can last for hours or days. Pain occurs with sexual contact, tampons, or even pressure from a bike seat. In some extreme cases, women feel this pain all the time.

Samantha only experienced it when attempting to have intercourse. Unable to enjoy sexual relationships and activities, Samantha shared that she felt that she had been cut off from the waist down and felt hopeless and depressed over her symptoms.

I started by asking her when she had started feeling the pain. She told me that it had coincided with a laser-based vaginal procedure and the onset of menopause. The pain had worsened with time. It also became clear that the pain began during a particularly low point in her primary romantic relationship. Samantha and her partner of many years, Stan, moved, leaving their support systems behind. Samantha explained that she felt as if a wall came down in their relationship at this point, and described it as a very dark period.

When an issue has been around a long time, as was the case with Samantha, there often is not one big trauma to work on, but a collection of events from the past. For Samantha, it wasn't one thing we worked on that held the key to her physical symptoms, but more an accumulation of events that had sent her body over the tipping point. After clearing a variety of events using the Tell the Story Technique, we spent time clearing her secondary gains around the problem, including her subconscious fear that if she healed 100%, she would have to go back to an overwhelming relationship with Stan.

We spent about 3 months working through all the events and gains. When I interviewed Samantha two years after we finished, she reported that she was still pain free. Although Samantha did not experience a "one-minute wonder," she said she experienced a miracle. Sometimes miracles take a while to attain.

Even if a person comes to you reporting that a chronic illness is pivotal in their lives, your sessions might turn out to be less focused on the illness and more focused on other issues and emotions. Always follow the lead of the client, as in the following case study.

Case Study: Cancer and Anger

This composite client story provides a good illustration of using EFT in working with cancer. Julie had a terminal disease and was told that the available treatments would only extend her life a few months. Her goal for coming to EFT was that she wanted the last of her life to be as calm and pain free as she could make it. She wanted to spend her remaining time enjoying her friends, children, and grandchildren, rather than feeling bad from chemo and radiation. She was comfortable with her choice.

Julie was a pleasant person who, in spite of her diagnosis, came into her session with a smile on her face. She reported that all her life she had been overly responsible. Additionally, she acknowledged that she was "wound tight," out of touch with her emotions, and believed it was not safe to express the emotions with which she was in touch. Cancer was the last straw. She lamented, "I realize now I have all this built-up anger, but I can't seem to express any of it."

Over several sessions, she dealt with the issues behind her inability to express anger and other emotions in a healthy way. Following is part of what came out of those sessions.

- **Stated Presenting Problem:** Unable to express anger or other emotions.

- **Reported intensity of inability to express emotions:** 9.

- When did this start? Who taught you that it was not safe to express feelings?

Julie's father was a controlling man who felt that children should be seen and not heard. She and her siblings were not allowed to "run around and be children." Her father could certainly express his anger, sometimes violently, but the children were not supposed to express any negative emotion. Nor, for that matter, were they supposed to express happy ones either, especially not noisy happy emotions. Although intense emotions were forbidden, the children were required to smile. "Put a smile on your face, kid," her papa, as Julie called him, would say. He usually added, "You have food and a roof over your head; you got nothing to be unhappy about."

So Julie had gone through life with a smile, no matter how she felt, locking her feelings way behind a façade created by the smile she wore continually. Because she believed it would be dangerous to express her anger, the Setup Statement was: *Even though I have all this anger and believe it would be dangerous to express it, I choose to deeply and completely accept how I feel.* Julie had a hard time saying that she accepted how she felt. She finally settled on…*I want to deeply and completely accept how I feel.*

Note: If you, or your clients, have a problem expressing the wording of an acceptance statement, just change it to something that you/they *can* accept. Remember that you are not being asked to accept everything about yourself forever after. Just accepting *something* about yourself *at this moment in time* is the relevant action. Because there is often a conflict between a part of you that accepts you as you are and a part that doesn't, Ann uses a Setup that incorporates both sides: "I accept the part of me that accepts myself and the part of me that doesn't."

While some practitioners simply tell their client to just "say it anyway," the authors believe that statement could legitimately invite resistance—conscious or unconscious. After all, who really likes to be told what to do? Our strong philosophy of "follow the client's lead" and client empowerment is better served by starting with an accurate but limited statement that the client accepts at that moment. Karin will often use "right here, right now, I'm okay." Most often, in a short time, after clients clear stuck energy, they become comfortable saying, "I deeply and completely accept myself."

Reminder Phrase at each point: *Dangerous to express anger.*

After tapping several rounds and reducing her intensity, Julie said, "Well, I guess in some situations it would not be dangerous." When asked, "Can you remember an event in which *it had* been dangerous, Julie replied that there were a several incidents [What happened? Who was involved?] of her, or another sibling, being sent to their room without supper, to, as her papa put it, "remember what you have to smile about." [What was the worst part about it? Going without supper or having your father upset and him blaming you for his being upset?] "Definitely upsetting my papa!" Julie said. [Is there one of those events that stand out?] Julie picked one. [When you think of it what would be the intensity?] "A seven."

Setup Statement: *Even though I upset Papa when I was feeling bad and not smiling, I accept myself anyway.* This time Julie felt okay saying the affirmation.

Reminder Phrase at each point: *Upsetting Papa.*

After two rounds, she stopped and said, "As a teenager, I realized that my father got very upset when anyone was not smiling because he *needed* us all to act happy all the time. It was like he believed he wasn't doing a good job." [That's great insight for teenaged Julie! How does that fit *now*?] Julie said, "That's just it! I loved my papa, I didn't want to hurt him. Somehow knowing why he was the way he was, made it even more important to be smiling all the time. I did not want him to feel like a failure. It's like it's my job, my responsibility even, to make him feel good."

The practitioner responded, "So are you saying it's your responsibility to keep him from feeling like a failure? What does that mean to you?" Julie sobbed, "He won't love me." This was a new aspect and a related core issue. This time tapping was begun without stopping to assess her intensity. Tears do not always mean that the intensity level is a 10, but the authors do not always initially stop to ask for an intensity level when the intensity is obviously very high and the client is upset.

Notice the Setup and Reminder Phrases that follow continued to use her words.

Setup Statement: *Even though Papa won't love me if I express anger, and I have to protect him from feeling like a failure, I deeply and completely accept myself.*

Reminder Phrases were created using the words from her story:

EB: *These tears.*

E: *Papa won't love me.*

UE: *Dangerous to express anger.*
UL: *It's my responsibility,*
Ch: *to make him feel good,*
CB: *to always be smiling.*
A: *I have to protect him.*
H: *Papa won't love me.*

After three rounds, Julie took a deep breath. As this is often a sign that there has been significant movement, the intensity was checked on "Papa won't love me." It was "about a 2."

Then checking the intensity of being unable to express emotions, her presenting problem, which began at a 9, Julie responded, "Well, I can see that there are places where I can safely express my emotions and I don't have to do it violently like Papa did, maybe a 4 now."

"And the 'Papa won't love you' part, what keeps it at a 2?"

"I think it's the part that it is my responsibility. I've always felt overly responsible for everything. I know it is irrational, but I feel like the people I love will feel bad about themselves, like my papa, if I don't act happy, stay smiling."

Notice that this belief is a different aspect of the "Papa won't love me" issue. Julie said she believed she was responsible for everyone's happiness and, although she consciously knew it was irrational, she felt that if she weren't happy, others would fall apart like her papa did. It occurred to her as she talked that she was afraid they, too, would become violent.

Setup Statement: *Even though I know it is irrational for me to have to act happy so the people around me will not feel bad, I deeply and completely accept myself.*

Reminder Phrases:

EB: *It seems irrational.*
E: *I know it is.*
UE: *I feel like I have to act happy*
UL: *no matter what.*
Ch: *I'm responsible*
CB: *for making sure they feel good.*
A: *I have to protect them.*
H: *It's irrational.*

And a couple more rounds:
EB: *I have to smile to be loved.*
E: *I'm responsible for their feelings.*
UE: *I have to act happy*
UL: *no matter what*
Ch: *or they will be violent*

CB: *like Papa.*
A: *I have to protect them.*
H: *It's irrational.*
EB: *I have to smile to be loved.*
E: *I'm responsible for their feelings.*
UE: *I have to act happy*
UL: *no matter what*
Ch: *or they will be violent*
CB: *like Papa.*
A: *I have to protect them*
H: *It's irrational.*

Julie took a deep breath. (Note the following cognitive shifts.) "Gosh, not only is it irrational, I'm acting like I control their emotions. I don't have that kind of power. On top of that they are not stupid. Just like I could tell when my papa really wasn't happy even if he was smiling and not violent. I bet they can tell when I'm worried or upset in spite of my smiles." She continued, "But I don't have any practice expressing my emotions in a healthy way. And I have no idea how to initiate a talk to them about my feelings. I didn't teach my children how to express and deal with emotions either."

Julie had just shared several more issues to address. At times, a client may need some information and/or a safe place to practice a new skill during a session. Such practice sessions are a useful way of discovering other involved aspects that could possibly prevent behavioral changes as you continue to address the presenting problem and decrease the emotions around related events. It is the practitioner's job to create a safe environment and relationship for the client to feel comfortable in expressing long-repressed emotions and in practicing new skills.

In further sessions, Julie focused on the intense anger she felt. She liked the concept of ranting and tapping. She liked just tapping and saying all those long-suppressed thoughts and emotions. At first, it took a little encouragement for her to say what she *really* felt and thought, no matter how unreasonable she judged it to be. After a few times of assuring her that this was a safe place to say whatever she felt, she really got into it. She tapped and tapped, at times yelling, until she couldn't think of anything else to say. She left that session with an honest smile on her face.

Julie joined a cancer support group and was encouraged to begin expressing her emotions with the members. She reported that the group had been very supportive and understanding. She also pointed out that, because she'd drained the "worst" emotions, she believed that she was well on her way to beginning to be able to talk to her kids. Additional sessions focused on her fears around sharing her real feelings with her children.

Death and Dying

The term "serious disease" can apply to a wide range of conditions, including but certainly not limited to chronic conditions, autoimmune disorders, and terminal illnesses such as cancer, heart disease, and Alzheimer's disease. Although many EFT practitioners might believe that the goal of working with clients who have serious diseases is to see them disease-free and living a life of health and prosperity, the reality is that this may not occur.

Often, when we think of EFT, we are focused on all the near-miraculous and inspiring success stories, of which there are many. There are times, however, when success might not look the way we want it to look. This is true of all EFT work. We, as practitioners, cannot be effective if we get caught up in what we believe "success" should be for any particular client. Ann uses the acronym NATO—not attached to the outcome—to bring home the concept that while we can care, often deeply, about our client, having our own agenda or outcome for the client is counterproductive for the client and gets in the way of deep work.

When we are working with clients who have serious, chronic, and terminal diseases, it is both fundamental and imperative to remember that we do not have the knowledge, the right, or the obligation to define success for anyone else. We are there to facilitate healing. That healing can take many forms, including assistance with family impact, alleviating side effects of allopathic treatment, accepting the diagnosis itself, reducing fear, learning to cope with pain, and much more.

Emma Roberts wrote an exceptionally helpful book, *Even Though I Have Cancer,* which is a must-read for any practitioner working with serious diseases. Her book includes strategies and techniques that, although focused on how to deal with many of the related issues associated with getting the diagnosis and then living with cancer, are also applicable to any disease. The book provides several case studies and useful tapping sequences containing what she has found are themes in working with cancer patients. One of those common threads among her patients is suppressed emotion, especially anger.

When working with serious diseases, it is important to address the emotions associated with having the disease, as well as suppressed emotions from events earlier in life. It is not critical, however, to find specific events to address with tapping. It is often useful to work with whatever specific emotion is being felt and/or expressed at the time. Emma has noted that emotions are often released in layers. "It's not always critical to know the when, where, or why of the emotion. If it's being released, just tap to assist it on its way, acknowledge it, and let it go. We don't always need to know the origins of things, often it is enough to just go with what presents itself in the moment" (Roberts, 2010, p. 66).

Emma has observed that tapping can help reduce the pain and the side effects of radiation. She wrote, "My clients found that by working to reduce the fear and anxiety around the treatment itself, side effects are lessened and the entire experience of treatment becomes a little easier" (Roberts, 2010, p. 50). "The goal is to respect the patient's individual journey, putting our own need for a particular outcome to one side [and] to allow that transition to be as peaceful and as beautiful as it is possible for it to be" (p. 379). The work completed by Emma's patients changed their lives, and probably also saved a few.

Tapping cannot stop the inevitable, however; we will all die. Although we can sometimes use tapping to help people avoid an untimely death, either through helping them reduce disease symptoms or even self-harm issues, eventually both clients and practitioners will need to face their own deaths and possibly other people's deaths. In earlier chapters in her book, Emma gives examples of working directly with the fear of death. In the last chapter, she discusses how to deal with the final stage of life—dying:

> When working with the transition from life to death start by working towards acceptance and a state of inner peace. Our role is merely to accompany the person on their soul's journey, preparing them as they place their trust in a Higher Self, whatever form that might take, and helping them let go of their physical being as they face the inevitability of death. This can be where the tapping is at its most pure, gently removing any remaining unspoken obstacles and allowing the patient to "be," accepting their spiritual self.

> Your role here is one of facilitator, merely to be there, gently tapping on their finger points. The power of the soft physical touch at this point is reassuring and is all that is needed, words no longer play a part. Allow yourself to be a bridge between this world and the next. At this point it is simply a case of gentle contact. Hopefully, pain relief will be being expertly managed, but tapping to reduce pain and discomfort can also help. (Roberts, 2010, pp. 379–383)

As a practitioner, you might be called upon to assist clients as they approach death. You might encounter clients for whom what you can do involves helping them be as comfortable as possible during their last weeks, days, or hours. Sometimes our compassionate presence is an incredible gift to people. Sometimes we can tap on ourselves as surrogates for people whose skin and muscles have become too sensitive to touch or tap on. Sometimes they want us to lay a hand on their hand while we tap on ourselves. Sometimes we can tap on them if they want to be tapped on but lack the strength to tap on themselves. Sometimes they want to talk and sometimes they want us to talk for them. The most important part of working with a client who is facing death or who is living with a life-threatening disease is to respect their wishes and follow their lead.

The death of a client does not mean that you have failed, and it does not mean that EFT didn't work. Ultimately, the success of EFT is still susceptible to any number of variables, including the progress of the disease, the general health and history of the client, whether the client is willing to do work on his or her own, the amount of work required as opposed to the amount of time the body has left, diet, sleep, and so on. Your success as a practitioner comes from your willingness to journey with your clients through their own work, offering them EFT, guidance, and support along the way. Ultimately, it is your clients who choose the direction of the path they take, or whether to use EFT at all.

Early on in Karin's practice, Dr. Patricia Carrington spoke with her regarding a client who had been told she had 2 months to live. Dr. Carrington asked, "Are you okay with the fact that she could die even though you worked with her?"

Karin answered, "I'm not working to keep her alive; my goal is to help her feel better. Of course, with all I've seen, I know it may be possible she can heal, but that's not up to me."

If you feel any reservations in working with clients who have chronic illnesses, then don't. Refer them to another practitioner. There are many people in the world in need of assistance with other issues. At the time of this writing, Kari is uncomfortable working with clients who have been diagnosed with a terminal illness. She chooses to refer those clients to others.

If a practitioner feels uncomfortable working with any specific client or any specific issue, the ethical recourse is to refer the client. You can tell the client that you are not experienced in x, but you can recommend others who would be better able to meet their needs. If you do not know anyone who would be better able to meet their needs, this is a time to reach out to anyone you do know who might work with this type of issue. Network. Talk to anyone you know who might know someone. We don't want to leave clients without resources and we generally have better skills at contacting people in the field than our clients have.

Advanced Trauma

In Chapter 9 of the *EFT Level 2 Comprehensive Training Resource,* you were introduced to the use of EFT with posttraumatic stress disorder (PTSD), which is a diagnosable syndrome that affects some individuals after they have experienced a trauma. Identifying PTSD, however, is only the tip of the physical, emotional, and psychological iceberg that is trauma as a whole. In this chapter, we would like to offer you a broader understanding of trauma and the variety of ways that it can manifest within the individual, as well as the ways in which EFT can play a significant role in reducing the effects of trauma.

You already know that EFT can be used to effectively address singular, traumatic events. But how is trauma understood when approached as an abstract concept, rather than as an adjective describing something else? The *Diagnostic and Statistical Manual of Mental Disorders,* 5th edition (DSM-5; American Psychiatric Association, 2013) categorizes trauma as exposure to: "death, threatened death, actual or threatened serious injury, or actual or threatened sexual violence as follows" (one required):

1. Direct exposure

2. Witnessing, in person.

3. Indirectly, by learning that a close relative or close friend was exposed to trauma. If the event involved actual or threatened death, it must have been violent or accidental.

4. Repeated or extreme indirect exposure to aversive details of the event(s), usually in the course of professional duties (e.g., first responders, collecting body parts; professionals repeatedly exposed to details of child abuse). This does not include indirect non-professional exposure through electronic media, television, movies, or pictures.

Although this definition is "generally accepted" because it is formally presented as representing the set of criteria that are selected by the committee that wrote the

DSM-V, this definition has been criticized for being too narrow. The issue of what types of experiences and events can be constituted as "traumatic" and what types cannot is an ongoing discussion in the field. This ongoing discussion has led to the emergence of a variety of definitions of trauma.

Some, including Esther Giller, president of the Sidran Institute for Traumatic Stress Education and Advocacy, define trauma much more loosely: "...the key to understanding traumatic events is that it refers to extreme stress that overwhelms a person's ability to cope" (Giller, 1999). Still others prefer definitions more similar to the earlier versions of the DSM, such as the 1980 definition, which maintains that trauma could only be represented by events outside the range of usual human experience.

The Experience and Perception of Trauma

Regarding EFT, as iterated in the previous two coursebooks, it is important to remember that the responsibility of differentiating between "traumatic" and "not traumatic" does not lie with the practitioner; rather, it is entirely dependent on the experience of the client. Jon Allen, author of *Coping with Trauma: A Guide to Self-Understanding* (1995) suggests that there are two components to trauma: the subjective and the objective. He writes:

> It is the subjective experience of the objective events that constitutes the trauma...The more you believe you are endangered, the more traumatized you will be...Psychologically, the bottom line of trauma is overwhelming emotion and a feeling of utter helplessness. There may or may not be bodily injury, but psychological trauma is coupled with physiological upheaval that plays a leading role in the long-range effects. (p. 14)

In other words, the definition of trauma, and the severity of it, originates in the perception and interpretation of the client. As you work with individuals who have experienced trauma and who are perhaps dealing with one or more of the many aftereffects of trauma, always begin with clients' perception and interpretation of their own experience. Two individuals could live through the same negative event, with one person feeling traumatized by the experience and the other person not. In the same way, you might find yourself working with clients who define particular experiences as traumatic when you might not previously have imagined that such an experience would be traumatic. In these types of situations, be mindful of where your clients are in their own experience. Work with the clients' perception and interpretation, rather than allowing your own interpretation of a particular event or experience to cloud the information coming from the client.

Trauma can be caused by a variety of types of events. Esther Giller (1999) writes that the Sidran Institute purposely defines trauma in a broad way, including responses to one-time incidents, chronic incidents, human-made experiences, natural disasters, and anything that overwhelms the individual's ability to cope. She writes, "[Our] definition intentionally does not allow us to determine whether a particular event is traumatic; that is up to each survivor."

Similarly, trauma specialist Dr. Robert Scaer (2006, p. 50) writes:

> ...any negative life event occurring in a state of relative helplessness—a car accident, the sudden death of a loved one, a frightening medical procedure, a significant experience of rejection—can produce the same neurophysiological changes in the brain as do combat, rape, or abuse. What makes a negative life event traumatizing isn't the life-threatening nature of the event, but rather the degree of helplessness it engenders—and one's history of prior trauma.

Here, Dr. Scaer suggests that the two main criteria for whether or not an event or experience is deemed traumatic are the individual's state of relative helplessness at the time of the experience and the individual's "storehouse of prior trauma."

These past traumas are significant because they can cause a smaller, less traumatic event, or sometimes an event that would not be traumatic at all under normal circumstances, to be experienced as highly traumatic. For example, if your client was involved in a serious car accident several years ago that involved being rear-ended by another driver and critically injured, another experience could be experienced as highly traumatic if it evokes memories, consciously or subconsciously, of the initial trauma.

Note that other people might not experience this second trauma (or even the first trauma) as equally traumatic as the person who was in the car accident experiences it. Sitting at a light and noticing, in the rearview mirror, that another driver is not paying attention and is taking too long to come to a stop, could induce intense feelings of fear and helplessness, even if no accident occurs. Similarly, a small fender bender in the parking lot could remind one of the original accident, heightening a person's stress response to the new event, even though many people would walk away from such an experience unaffected.

Issue Strings and Trauma Triggers

When addressing trauma with EFT, be aware of these types of potential connections. You will probably hear a variety of terms used to describe these connected issues. Karin calls them "issue strings," as a way of reminding her trainees that traumatic events and experiences don't always stand alone. Sometimes they are tied to one previous experience and sometimes they are tied to a host of previous experiences. When working to resolve an experience that is traumatic, you may find it necessary to explore and treat earlier similar or related events to find the actual trigger.

In EFT trainings, Ann and Karin like to have the attendees switch seats on the second day. Having a different visual perspective and sitting next to different peo-

81

ple often helps them grasp concepts they might previously had problems under-standing. In one such training, a woman moved to a different seat but before sitting down closed the drapes. Another woman, Wendy, became extremely upset, and in a panicked voice, yelled, "Don't close the drapes!" Then, pulling out sunglasses and obviously trying to calm down, she spoke more softly, "I need natural light. I'd have to wear sunglasses without natural light."

Exasperated, the woman who closed the drapes replied, "But the lights are on in here." It was clear that Wendy was close to tears. "I just need them open, okay!" Wendy was in such an obviously panicked state that the woman who had closed the drapes reopened them and moved to a different seat. Others in the class were shaking their heads and appeared perplexed about Wendy and her reaction.

Karin asked, "Do you think Wendy *means* to be annoying to anyone? She was clearly panicking." Karin continued, "Wendy, do you know why you were so afraid?" When Wendy answered that she had no idea and that her fear had plagued her for years, Karin explained to the class, "There is a *reason* why Wendy is reacting like this. Something happened in her past that is now being triggered. EFT can be used to help find out when this started and then help to clear the associated learned response. Wendy, I invite you to use some of our breakout practice sessions to find the core event."

During one of the practice sessions, Wendy suddenly said, "I know! I remem-ber!" More than a decade ago, Wendy had been in a very bad car accident and she remembered that in the ambulance there was a large, very bright fluorescent light right above her. She had begged the EMS technicians to turn down the light, but they said they couldn't.

Karin used Wendy's story to help the class understand how traumatic experi-ences can be linked to later smaller events, triggering a reaction that seems illogical. "Wendy was triggered even though she didn't know why. She panicked and each of you witnessed it. She knew it wasn't logical and certainly didn't mean to freak out. There is always a reason. As practitioners you seek to find the event(s) that creat-ed the trigger. You clearly have to rely on clients to discover their own triggering events (with your help) because you would never in a million years guess what was related to what. Our goal is to understand the clients' way of reacting, thinking and feeling. Wendy unknowingly gave a wonderful example of how even small triggers can generate a reaction that seems on the surface totally illogical and disconnected to the current event."

The woman who had originally shut the drapes said, "Oh my goodness, I am so sorry. I thought you were just being ridiculous. I feel so terrible. What a lesson, thank you!" Others in the class apologized as well. Wendy revealed that this has been happening for 11 years. She couldn't go into a mall without sunglasses, she couldn't go into restaurants after dark, she couldn't go to the theatre because of the stage lights, and more. Karin later worked with Wendy to complete the work done in class; fluorescent lights are no longer a problem.

Addressing trauma can be as straightforward as working directly on the emotions derived from the original event or it can be highly complicated, depending on the nature and scope of the trauma. Trauma can exist in many complex layers. In his 2005 presentation at the Fifth International Congress for System Constellations, clinical psychologist Fred Gallo, PhD, iterated the importance of addressing trauma on multiple levels. He spoke about a conscious attachment to trauma and an unconscious attachment to trauma.

Conscious attachment to trauma refers to the *explicit memory* of the event and meaning. This would include one's ability to consciously recall facts or events, often in a narrative form. Unconscious memory of a trauma refers to the *implicit memory* of the event, which is the part of one's memory that is not currently available to conscious recall. Implicit memory can include information stored in energy systems, information specifically suppressed or repressed so the conscious mind is unaware of it, as well as body recall, sometimes referred to as sensorimotor memory. Dr. Gallo maintains that implicit memory is more significant than explicit memory.

Nonetheless, most times, it is the conscious recall of an event that will provide you, as an EFT practitioner, the starting line for addressing a trauma. From that starting position, you can do the work required to unpack and address all the complex layers that can exist within trauma.

Traumatic Memory

In all three books in this series, we have addressed concepts and issues related to working with memory. Fortunately, practitioners can work with memories without being able to understand at a neurophysiological level exactly what memories are or how they work. The relationship between memory and trauma is still widely debated. The idea that traumatic experiences can alter or impede memory function was introduced in the early 19th century (Uttl, Ohta, & Siegenthaler, 2006, p. 259). Since then, theories of traumatic memory, somatic expressions of traumatic memory, repression, and dissociation concerning traumatic memories have been widely explored by psychologists, neurologists, and scientists alike.

Several schools of thought have emerged from this exploration of human memory and trauma. Many professionals support the idea that a traumatic experience causes memory distortion. Some have suggested that these memories are stored in a different part of the brain than nontraumatic memories are, while others do not differentiate, from a neurophysiological point of view, between traumatic memories and any other memory. Nonetheless, clinical data since 1919 have demonstrated a direct correlation between trauma and memory disturbance (Giller, 1999; Van der Kolk, 1994).

Although data substantiating these ideas might prove difficult to recreate in a standard laboratory environment, we will approach traumatic memory as a distinct phenomenon. We suggest that trauma can alter how a memory is stored and recalled, as well as result in several, sometimes serious, emotional and somatic responses.

Human memory is an incredibly complex phenomenon, and is further complicated when one experiences trauma. Researchers generally agree that there are two forms of memory—implicit and explicit—and four stages of memory. These stages are: intake, storage (encoding), rehearsal, and retrieval (Sidran Institute and Enoch Pratt Health System, 1994). The efficacy of these processes can be greatly affected by a number of factors, including the type or degree of trauma, environment, developmental stages, expectations or experiences after the event occurs, plus other factors. According to the Sidran Institute, single-event traumas, trauma caused by natural or accidental causes, and trauma experienced by those who received validation and support after the occurrence are more likely to be remembered explicitly (1994). In contrast, the Sidran Institute also suggests that repetitive or multi-event traumas, those with a deliberate human cause, traumas experienced by children, and traumatic experiences with undertones of denial or secrecy are more likely to result in memory disturbance.

Memory disturbance among trauma victims can be manifested in a variety of ways. These include: amnesia or disassociation, fragmentation (in which clients only remember bits and pieces of an event), lack of clarity, and intense somatic responses (in which clients have little or no conscious recall of the event but experience a high degree of related bodily reactions). There is scientific evidence that, unlike standard memories, traumatic memories are stored in the part of the brain known as the limbic system (Sidran Institute and Enoch Pratt Health System, 1994).

The limbic system processes emotions and sensations but does not process language or speech. For this reason, many people who experienced traumatic events developed some type of memory disturbance that can lead to vivid implicit awareness of the feelings generated by the traumatic experience, or awareness of the body sensations related to the traumatic event, but have limited explicit narrative memories with which to explain these reactions. Thankfully, EFT provides trauma sufferers with a tool to address their traumatic memories, regardless of how distorted or fragmented they are, and regardless of how clearly or vaguely they are remembered.

When it comes to individuals who have experienced trauma, EFT can be used to address whatever memory and sensations are available, and whatever information and emotions the EFT process evokes. As practitioners, we are not concerned with the actual facts of the event, but rather with the emotional impact and clients' perceptions. (Note, however, there have been anecdotal warnings that using EFT to address memories can so alter one's perception of the events that it could possibly interfere with one's ability to recall the specifics of the event and affect one's ability to testify in legal proceedings.)

Just as beauty is in the eye of the beholder, trauma is often in the eye of the traumatized individual. Actually, qualities of beauty, trauma, attractiveness, or challenge do not reside in external things, events, or situations. We, as humans, through our interpretations of things, events, or situations, determine what is beautiful, what is ugly, what is traumatizing, what is challenging, what is fun, what is boring, and so forth. That is why 100 of us could be exposed to the same thing, event, or situation and we could have 100 different reactions to that experience. In reality, among the 100 of us, we would probably have 10 to 20 different primary reactions, although it would be possible for us to have 100 different reactions. We humans are really that varied and we can be that individually distinct.

Researchers seeking to understand how traumatic memory works in the human brain have suggested that traumatic memory can intrude upon and influence new experiences, much like the example of Wendy and fluorescent lights. When information from these traumatic memories intrudes on one's consciousness in new situations, it can trigger the past event, cognitively, emotionally, or physically.

For example, if client, Sarah, is sexually assaulted by her boss, the traumatic memory from this experience can corrupt other experiences, even years later. She may experience cognitive flashbacks when working with other authority figures who are male, she might find herself clenching her jaw or experiencing unexplained anxiety when alone in a room with a man, or she might find herself experiencing flashbacks or vivid memories of her experience when standing in a elevator with a man who is wearing the same cologne as her previous boss. These feelings—both physical and emotional—are generally the same feelings she experienced at the time of the trauma. Although the event is not literally repeating in real life, her body and emotions might react as if it is happening right now, regardless of the amount of time that has passed.

The amount of time that has passed is not relevant because emotional memories are not rooted in time or place; they are rooted in our experiences and our bodies. Until they are resolved, they can come screaming back at us as if they are happening right now this minute. Our hearts race; our breathing becomes erratic; our muscles tense. We are on edge, even if we don't remember why. It's about safety. People experiencing trauma no longer feel safe in specific, or even more broadly defined situations, and the body responds in a variety of ways. Our bodies remember for us and warn us to be careful. Our bodies and our reactions warn us to watch out for tigers or snakes in the jungle, shrieking tires skidding on pavement on the highway, flashing lights in the city, or curtains that are being closed, leaving us exposed to fluorescent lights.

EFT is such an incredibly valuable tool when working with trauma because EFT allows us to address the original traumatic event in its entirety. By resolving original fears and interpretations, we help clients give themselves permission to release these triggered responses. In many cases, these triggered responses have significantly disrupted the lives of those who have experienced trauma.

More recent research in the area of human memory has suggested that memories are rewritten every time they are recalled. This phenomenon of rewriting memories is termed "memory reconsolidation." It is based on the idea that, when a memory is retrieved, it enters a state of vulnerability in which it can be reevaluated, rewritten, or even replaced. Neuroscientist Daniela Schiller suggests that recent research, including her own, "has shown that memories are not unchanging physical traces in the brain. Instead, they are malleable constructs that may be rebuilt every time they are recalled" (Hall, 2013).

Schiller, along with her colleagues at Mount Sinai School of Medicine at New York University, and other notable researchers have compiled an impressive amount of data suggesting that humans can "alter the emotional impact of a memory by adding new information to it or recalling it in a different context" (Hall, 2013). Furthermore, Schiller believes that these findings suggest the efficacy of "radical non-pharmacological approaches to treating pathologies like posttraumatic stress disorder, other fear-based anxiety disorders, and even addictive behaviors" (Hall, 2013).

Schiller's groundbreaking research explains that it is possible to alter one's emotional response to memories, even though clients can still recollect the events. As clients release their stuck emotions, when they tell the narrative about what happened, their descriptions of what happened change. They omit some details that were once important but no longer seem important, and add other details that at one point they had forgotten but now remember. Narratives that were once delivered with intense emotions have sometimes become so resolved that clients are now almost bored with narratives that they used to tell over and over to anyone who would listen.

The recent research on memories is significant because it challenges the widely accepted view of memory established in the early 20th century, which suggested that memories, while fragile at the time of formation, were strengthened over time and permanently stored in the brain (Hall, 2013). Modern research, such as that by Schiller, however, has found that memories are initially encoded in the part of the brain known as the hippocampus and then sent, by means of biochemical and electrical signals, to other parts of the brain for storage, depending on the type and function of the memory. Essentially, these memories can be accessed or triggered, and each time one is brought to the forefront, new information and perspectives are added, allowing the memory to be rewritten based on the current context of the recall.

Memory does not exist as an unchanging file in our brains, but as a series of rewrites based on the most recent recollection of the scenario. This process is more similar to heating glass and forming it into a shape, such as a bottle, bowl, or vase. Unlike clay, which once it is fired remains rigid thereafter, once glass is formed, it remains forever mutable (changeable). That is, if a glass product is reheated, it can be reformed into a new shape. Glass will not take a new shape unless it is reheated, but reheating allows it to be reshaped.

Similarly, clients might have remembered a trauma repeatedly without releasing the uncomfortable or miserable memories associated with the trauma. In that case, they might believe that their memories of the event are unchanging. That would be similar to pressing on a cold glass item and despairing of it ever changing its shape. Until the glass item is heated, it will not change! Tapping is a process that allows, encourages, and supports clients to change, just as heat provides the necessary environmental factor for glass to be safely and effectively altered in shape.

In 2012, MIT neuroscientists Xu Liu and Steve Ramirez took significant steps in expanding our understanding of how memory works. By identifying the areas of the brain where memories are stored, they were able to observe and manipulate the memory experience of mice. In their study of false memories, researchers discovered further evidence that memories are stored in a network of neurons (Trafton, 2013). Their work demonstrated that if the neurons that contained a particular memory were stimulated, the mouse's brain would respond as if the memory were actually occurring, even if the environment in which the mouse was currently located was unrelated to that memory.

Mice were placed in a box and given a mild electric shock; they formed a memory of this negative event. The next day when the mice were placed in a second, unrelated box, they exhibited the normal behavior of investigating a new enclosure. When the researchers stimulated the neurons that held the previous, traumatic memory, the mice reacted as they did when the shock was administered in the previous box. This occurred even though the original negative memory was associated with the first box, and the second situation represented an entirely new environment that was completely benign.

This research, although it is still being developed, is highly significant for EFT and other energy-based approaches regarding resolving trauma. EFT offers a tool for directing the reconsolidation of memories that had been associated with traumatic events, sometimes referred to as rewriting traumatic memories, by resolving the emotional signature of those initially traumatic memories. If the emotional triggers and aspects can be resolved, reconsolidation can occur, thereby changing or erasing the negative effect traumatic memory has on one's daily life, and potentially eliminating symptoms such as flashbacks, somatic responses to emotional memory, or distressing emotions that appear to arise from nowhere.

Addressing Trauma with EFT

EFT has an extensive and well-documented history of being used to address trauma. It can bring immediate relief from traumatic memories and related symptoms. It can also act as a "gentle tool for revealing the many layers and aspects that may be connected with trauma, working through them systematically and effectively until their emotional charge has gone" (Roberts, 2013). We have already discussed how trauma can manifest as a singular, one-time event or as a larger, more amorphous condition caused by a series or accumulation of events or experiences. EFT Master Emma Roberts describes trauma within the context of four presenting categories. These are:

1. Prolonged Past Traumatic Experiences: Trauma experienced over a long period of time that is no longer occurring in the present. An example is having endured ongoing abusive episodes as a child.

2. Ongoing Trauma: Trauma experienced over a long period of time that is still occurring in the present. An example is constant threats to one's safety due to living in dangerous circumstances such as a war zone or neighborhoods where there is frequent street violence.

3. One-Time Trauma: Trauma that is experienced within the confines of one, singular event. An example is an automobile accident or someone's sudden death.

4. Perceived Trauma: Trauma that is experienced in a secondary manner, usually by witnessing the traumatic event via the media, friends, stories, etc. This also includes the trauma that can come from being an EFT practitioner and hearing people tell their traumatic experiences. We will address this further in the book, but it is important to remember to address any lingering emotions and perspectives that can come from experiencing the trauma of others through their stories. An example is the many people after the 9/11 event in New York City who experienced this sort of secondary trauma even though they were in a safe place and were physically untouched by the event.

The good news is that regardless of the type of trauma your client is experiencing, or has experienced, EFT provides an effective tool with which to address it.

In all cases, remember that clients have the necessary information regarding the trauma, and clients are the ones whose perspective determines which events and experiences are traumatic and which are not. The representation of the event or events stored in clients' memory might not be entirely accurate, so if you had a time machine and returned to view the original event, clients' memories might not serve effectively as a documentary regarding the event. For example, their memories could be vague, highly symbolic, exaggerated, unclear, or hyper-realistic.

We discussed earlier how reacting to trauma invites people to change or distort memory; memories are recalled and rewritten through the lens of the individual's perspective. Because historical accuracy is not the goal, but helping clients resolve trauma is the goal, we work with the information clients provide. As a practitioner, your job is to ensure your client's readiness and feeling of safety and to help them to a resolution that is beneficial for them, in their own space and *in their own time*.

Pay attention to even very small details of the event: the key factor in the trauma could be an unexpected, at least to you, detail. Help clients go over every detail of what they saw, heard, felt, smelled, or tasted. In an accident, it could be the smell of the rubber of the tires. Regarding the traumatic death of a loved one, it could be the monitor numbers in the intensive care unit flattening out, leading to that shrill sound associated with flat-lining, when all the jiggling lines on the screen that should be dynamically fluctuating suddenly cease.

In an ongoing trauma situation, it could be fear that the door would come crashing in, that another bomb would fall, that one more person would become ill, that quiet footsteps would be heard in the middle of the night leading to your room, or the sound of someone popping open another bottle that would signal trouble. With one of Ann's clients, it was the posture of the two people standing looking at the child that was interpreted as the most negative aspect by the client.

While working with a client, Kari experienced an example of how trauma, and the perspective through which traumatic memories are viewed, can alter the content and accuracy of a memory. Her client, a 45-year-old woman we will call Mary, was seeking resolution regarding a series of traumatic events concerning her mother. She told a story in which she, as a very young child, was inadvertently left at home alone.

Mary described abruptly waking up in the middle of the night and getting out of bed when she saw that there were lights on downstairs. As she walked down the hall, she noticed that the house was particularly quiet and had a strange feeling, especially since her parents had been entertaining other couples earlier that evening. Checking her parent's bedroom on the way down the hall and finding it empty, she continued downstairs, through the empty living room, the likewise empty dining room, and then went to the empty kitchen, discovering that the back door was left open and there was blood spattered all over the kitchen. She screamed and ran out of the room, but no one was home to hear her.

Using the EFT Tell the Story Technique, Kari invited her client to communicate whenever she felt a rise in emotion, at which point, they would stop and tap on the aspects of that piece of the event. Kari helped her client address all the aspects and decrease the intensity behind them, including the eerie feeling in the house when she woke up, the nervousness induced by the out-of-place silence in the house, the panic of not being able to find her parents, the sight of the open back door, the sight of the blood, the contrast between the bright red blood and the white kitchen surfaces, the fear and panic when she realized what she was looking at, the desperation of not knowing where to go, the feelings of abandonment at being left alone, the anger at her parents for not thinking of her, and so on.

After working through all presented aspects, Kari asked her client to recount the story one more time, paying extra attention to any spikes in emotion or unaddressed feelings that surfaced. Not only did Mary report that she experienced no emotional spikes when recalling the memory, but also, with the traumatic aspects of the memory addressed and resolved with EFT, she shared that she was sure her parents had only run to the house of a neighbor who was a registered nurse after someone had cut themselves with a knife in the kitchen, and that the "kitchen spattered with blood" was, to her surprise, only a small amount of blood on the table and some drips on the floor. When the traumatic aspects of a memory are addressed and resolved with EFT, the content of the memory might also change. In actuality, history did not change. What happened, happened, but when clients change the perspective through which they filter their memories, they can change their memories.

Not all clients will present with a specific memory in mind and a story to tell. Some present with physiological symptoms: migraines, serious diseases, stomach issues, and so on. Clients might not have made the connection between their physical experience and their past or ongoing traumatic experience. When that happens, and it happens more as a rule than as an exception, practitioners and clients have an opportunity to demonstrate their detective skills, their analytical skills, and their attention to detail. Some clients will be so overwhelmed by the need to tell their story that they forget to tap, or they want to skip the traditional EFT protocol altogether. As you have learned previously, in these situations, encourage clients to tap while they tell their story, or, with their permission, tap on them while they tell their story. The act of tapping as they share their story can be extremely powerful and profound.

It is helpful to already have options that can make it easier for your clients to participate in their own healing when they're having trouble with the typical protocol. For example, some people prefer not to tap on themselves, but would tap on a stuffed animal. One practice used by some practitioners, and the authors, is to keep various stuffed animals with buttons or marks on their bodies where the typical tapping points are located. Clients can select which animal to tap on. Allowing clients to select the animal they want to tap on is another step in empowering clients, as some clients come to us feeling disempowered in many parts of their lives. As children, their power was taken from them by someone, or as adults, they found themselves in situations where they lacked the wisdom, knowledge, or power to cope effectively with what happened. EFT allows clients to take back their legitimate power over their emotions, their bodies, and their reactions.

Sometimes, though, prior to taking back their power, clients feel vulnerable. They often feel vulnerable in life and they may feel vulnerable in our sessions, even if we strive to provide a warm, accepting, compassionate, and safe physical and emotional environment. While clients are still feeling vulnerable, some of them want to hold or hug a stuffed animal or let it sit in their laps while they tap. In offices where there are no stuffed animals, sometimes clients grab pillows and hold them. Soothing comes in a variety of ways. We do our clients and ourselves a favor to remember how uncomfortable it can be as we work to bravely face things we have not previously wanted to face.

The "Let's Pretend" Technique

Some clients have detached themselves from their traumatic experiences. This is the mind's natural coping response to situations and memories that it has deemed "unsafe." Detachment can present on a variety of levels. In some cases, clients will have no difficulty remembering the event but do not access any emotion concerning the event or memory. For example, clients might recite a story as if it involved someone else, or as if it is boring or meaningless. Occasionally, clients might laugh at themselves, at the situation, and at anyone who is emotionally distressed by what happened. Some clients might report a general feeling of discomfort, depression, or anxiety without any specific trauma or memory attached.

Whether clients are detached from their memories or not, or whether they are detached from their emotions or not, in all situations, encourage your clients to begin with whatever information is available to find a core issue or event. Remember that if your clients are unable to recall the specifics of a traumatic experience or event, or if they are unable to access a memory at all, or if all the events were so similar they cannot pick just one, you can encourage them to make up the details of a hypothetical experience.

Karin calls the exercise of having clients make up the details of an event "Let's Pretend." This can be a useful technique when working with clients who cannot remember the specifics of a particular event. It's beneficial for clients who have experienced significant trauma to which they developed some level of detachment or dissociation, and also for clients who have trouble accessing memories from early childhood or in general. The merits of the concept are the same for either group.

We have already discussed how the human brain often works in metaphors. In the same way, this metaphoric tendency allows the mind to work much like an Internet search engine. To put it simply, if someone were to say the phrase "bird on a fence," your mind "Googles" that phrase, recalling potentially hundreds of images and instances in which "bird on a fence" has been experienced. The mind then chooses the image or instance that can be applied most effectively to the context of the current experience. All of this occurs in a millisecond without any conscious realization. Essentially, this is what allows current events to trigger past emotional states and responses. This explains why clients are triggered so quickly and seemingly "out of nowhere." People are never triggered out of nowhere or for no reason. People are triggered for reasons that they do not accurately detect at the moment.

Sigmund Freud and his contemporaries, including Carl Jung, proposed that the information held in the subconscious, although not always readily accessible, is vitally important to the success of significant therapeutic intervention. They began to recognize, as evidenced in techniques such as free association and active imagination, that fantasy and dream states could be used to gain access to and potentially use subconscious material. There are some significant differences, however, between psychoanalysis and EFT. One of the primary differences is that psychoanalysts interpreted the information provided by their clients. If clients rejected their therapists' interpretations, these clients were deemed "resistant," and the focus of the therapy could shift to clients' resistance (Safran, 2012).

EFT does not in any way, shape, or form encourage practitioners to interpret what their clients are saying or experiencing. That is the role of the client. Practitioners might occasionally offer their guess or suggestion about what a client is intending to convey, but these are offered with the intention of providing clients with something they can accept to expand their position or can reject. Either reaction would be appropriate and could set the stage for the next "round." Clients give meaning to their reactions, their emotions, their beliefs, and their perspectives.

Psychoanalysts were the first to realize that people do have some access to their subconscious selves. In allowing clients to free-associate, psychoanalysts allowed clients to notice things about themselves and their reactions that they had previously kept hidden from themselves.

In the same way, "Let's Pretend" allows clients who have little or no access to memories to make up a story that 1) applies to the issue at hand, and 2) is both reasonable and feasible for them to use in addressing subconscious material. The subconscious mind will search to develop the story and to make the appropriate applications, while the conscious mind is free to relax without the stress and pressure of trying to recall memories that seem impossible to remember.

After a reasonable and feasible story is made up, with a beginning, middle, and an end, and after all the participants have been identified, it can be addressed using EFT *as if it actually happened.* "Let's Pretend," or making the request to "just make it up," can be applied to an entire memory or used to "fill in the blanks" if your client can only remember pieces of a memory.

Why does it work to use EFT with clients' made-up stories? Don't we have to have the whole truth of what happened? For example, when families or couples go to counseling, they often want to argue intensely over "what really happened," so the counselor can see their perspective. In reality, regardless of "what really happened," people react to events in their own way. They develop perspectives based on their experiences, personalities, and histories. In EFT, we help people release stuck energy and reconnect to parts of themselves from which they have become disconnected. This means that it's not the story that matters; it's the person who matters. Each person developed a perspective and a belief system with which we can work. In EFT, we are not working with history. We are working with people.

Case Study of "Let's Pretend"

John came to a session with Ann saying he was unable to sleep, was consumed with guilt, and felt like a total failure because he had been unable to protect his family. Two months previously, his son was hit with a baseball bat during a game. When his wife went running down to the field to help him, she tripped, breaking her leg. Medics were right there, treated his son's bruised arm and took his wife to the hospital to treat her leg. John and his son followed in their car but were not allowed to ride in the ambulance.

John believed that his current reaction was unrealistic to the situation. Now 2 months later, he reported that he was still experiencing "over-the-top panic," helplessness, and intense guilt. He explained that, although he understood logically that it was an accident and he was not responsible, he also felt strongly that he "should have been able to stop it." In the course of four or five sessions, Ann and John worked on both his physical manifestation of his emotions and all the details around the accident. They also worked on a couple of previous situations in which panic, guilt, and helplessness were key factors.

John's overall "10 plus," as he had initially called it, had dropped to a 3. He said, "I am very calm now as I think about the accident, but I still have this irrational sense of guilt and helplessness; I cannot seem to let it go." He could not recall any other situations in which those feelings predominated. Ann asked John to just close his eyes, take a slow breath, let his mind wander, and make up a possible story.

John smiled, "You're going to think I'm nuts, but I see myself as a cave-man." John gave significant details about a raid on his tribe. The invaders overran the village. He had hidden "his woman and baby" in a ditch covered by limbs he had pulled over them. John did a sharp intake of breath and said, "The raiders stabbed the baby!" John appeared totally shocked, saying, "And, then they rode off with 'my woman.'" He described how he helplessly watched what was happening, then ran as fast as he could after them, to no avail.

Present-day John opened his eyes and started to cry. All the feelings of panic, helplessness, and guilt came back in force. He exclaimed, "I should have been there. I should have been able to stop it." As John worked through all the aspects of this painful story involving the ancient cave family, he became calm and said, "What a sad story, I wonder where that came from? But I do feel detached from it now. Even in my story, I did the best I could. I also did the best I could with my son and wife around the accident."

During the next two sessions, John said he was sleeping well now, even though he had discovered a few additional aspects to resolve. In a six-month follow-up visit with Ann, John said the baseball accident was a still a non-issue.

Where did the story of the raiders come from? It doesn't matter. Whether it was fantasy, his version of a story he'd heard/read/seen in a movie, a metaphoric way he could accept dealing with his own internal fears, or a past life, it was a story that elicited strong emotional and bodily reactions from John. Whether you or your client believes there are past-life influences is definitely not the issue. Work with whatever the client presents. We do not need to have deep philosophical debates with our clients about what is "real."

Remember that what clients remember as real sometimes changes as they process their emotions; memories can, and do, change.

Proceeding Safely

Just as there are some clients who are dissociated, distant, or detached from their traumatic memories, other clients are absolutely enmeshed with their traumatic memories. They might have difficulty gaining distance or separating themselves from these traumas. In such cases, safety and going at the client's readiness pace is paramount. In some instances, clients might be afraid to address a particular issue because it feels unsafe or too intense, or they say they don't want to remember or revisit that memory. This may mean that you need to slow down. Spend more time developing rapport with these clients; work on less intense issues so that if and when they are ready, they know they are in an environment where they can safely unpack their trauma.

It's not always necessary to start tapping right away. Wait to start tapping until the client is ready, until you have established rapport and a feeling of safety for the client. This may take some time. Also, don't think you should always start with the most painful memory. Allow your client the time and space to explore and learn about the positive effects of tapping by beginning to tap on an issue or memory that is less intense. When clients experience success in dealing with minor issues, they develop the confidence and competence to tackle harder issues.

We want to stress that it is entirely okay to *not tap* at certain times. Pay more attention to the pace and safety of your clients than to how well you, as a practitioner, are getting them to tap and resolve their issues. Sessions are about clients, not about practitioners. Note that clients have the right, the option, and the choice to decide never to go back and address one specific issue or all their issues. It's their session and their life. We don't tell other people how and when to make their decisions. We respect their decisions, and their timing; this means we respect their unwillingness to deal with their vulnerabilities even though we might want them to make a different choice.

Take your cues from your clients; always meet them where they are in their process. They might be willing to begin simply by tapping globally on their fear or not tapping at all until they become comfortable with you and feel safe enough to address their deeper issues.

Occasionally, clients are as worried about someone else's issues as they are about their own issues. Sometimes when clients talk about how much they want someone else to "do their work," we can point out the reality that clients have an opportunity to be role models regarding the benefits of actually doing one's work. This means that if these clients do the work they came to us to do, people in their lives might want to know why they now look less burdened, smile more, or generally seem happier.

We, as practitioners, have the opportunity to be role models for our clients by telling them about something we struggled with when we first began doing this work. It's not that we want to tell clients all our thoughts, fears, and concerns; that would be excessive and unprofessional. It's that we want them to understand that we're all in the same boat in life. We all have issues and we all don't exactly want to face our issues. When we reveal in *general* terms things we used to struggle with but no longer struggle with because we have done our own work, we are opening a reasonable and familiar line of communication.

For example, we might say, "I used to be too scared to stand in front of a roomful of people, but doing EFT helped me realize that the audience is just made up of regular people and I'm not afraid anymore." We could say, "I used to get angry (sad, depressed, jealous, whatever), but by doing EFT, I learned how to manage my emotions rather than feeling as if I were being run over by them." Clients benefit when we share general aspects about ourselves (Bridges, 2001). To be therapeutically beneficial, the point of sharing information about ourselves is to offer support to our clients. Such personal stories from the practitioner need to be relevant to the client's particular issue or situation.

There are, of course, limits as to what you want to share with your client. When you, as a practitioner, are "just dying" to tell somebody about something, call a friend, family member, or your own practitioner. Your client is not the right person to fulfill this need. Common sense should tell you not to share these type of stories with clients. You are there to meet their needs, not to have clients meet yours. Then too, there are certain subjects that are generally not beneficial for clients to hear about. For example, telling clients about inappropriate fantasies you have is not likely to enhance the therapeutic alliance you have with them (Fisher, 2004).

If clients are hesitant or afraid to get close to a specific memory or experience, or the trauma of a particular memory is particularly intense or high, the Gentle Techniques might be appropriate. Allow clients to address the memory or event with as much distance as they need. In the Tearless Trauma Technique, as described in Level 1, you can encourage clients to identify a specific event and guess at what their emotional intensity might be if they were to choose to look at the event/movie in detail. This method is one way to give clients a safe and effective place to begin to address traumatic events.

After clients have guessed at the intensity of the specific event they chose, have them develop a title or phrase for the event and proceed with the EFT protocol. As you tap on the hypothetical intensity, levels will often drop. Through questions, you can gauge clients' readiness to address an actual movie of the event. Ask clients to guess at the intensity again, and compare the second guess to the first. Once clients' hypothetical intensity is down to an acceptably low level (e.g., if using the SUD scale, a 3 or below), you can invite them to actually imagine the incident. Rather than asking clients to go directly to issues they may find overly painful to address, beginning with distance and with guesses helps reduce some of the initial emotional intensity.

Being flexible in how you apply the gentle techniques and how you approach trauma with your clients can help ensure that your client feels safe at all times. Some clients might need even more distance than a movie screen can offer them.

95

If greater distance and more control are necessary for some clients to feel safe in the process, then feel free to alter the standard EFT approach to meet their needs. Clients who have experienced multiple or ongoing traumas often need to process memories slowly; at times, it really is okay to stop when the intensity has gone from a 10 to a 5. That can signal a huge change in the client that needs time to process. As Ann stresses to her students, "Sometimes the fastest way to get there is to slow down."

Some clients need a place to put the traumatic memory, as if the memory is being taken from being front and center to being put far away in a safe place so that clients experience a necessary and significant distance from the event. Dr. Lynn Karjala (2007) calls the emotional spaces that offer this type of distance "containment tools." She invites her clients to create a space with a variety of levels of containment for traumatic memories that have differing levels of intensity. She suggests thinking of "traumatic material as equivalent to radioactive waste and needing the same level of safety precautions" (p. 61). This safe space offers clients somewhere to store their traumatic memories between sessions and until those memories are ready to be addressed. Having a safe space to store and leave the painful material until clients are ready to address it can function as a strategy that offers the ultimate amount of distance to clients who are experiencing significant difficulty getting close to a traumatic memory.

Ultimately, the "safe space" can be anything that your clients experience as providing the greatest comfort. This could be a chest, a box, a hole in the ground, or it could even be created on another planet. Whatever makes them feel the most secure and allows them the distance they need to begin to consider addressing their memory is a suitable safe space.

Be aware of your client's needs as you help them address traumatic memories. Help your clients understand that they can create a long-term safe space or one that they only need to use for 5 minutes. The length of time a safe space is utilized will vary widely from one client to another.

The "safe space" can also be used as a metaphor for an issue being addressed. In the following case study, EFT Master Gwyneth Moss allows her client as much distance as she needs by placing the memory in a can in the darkest part of her basement cupboard. The can in the cupboard allows Gwyneth's client the distance she needs from the issue she fears to address. The can and cupboard in this story are not meant to contain or store the traumatic material indefinitely, but they offer temporary distance to help the client feel safer until she is ready to address the issue at hand.

Case Study:
Fear of Addressing the Big Issue

In her 10-disc *EFT Helps* DVD set, EFT Master Gwyneth Moss works with a variety of clients who are dealing with some form of trauma. In one of these sessions, client Rosie begins the session in clear emotional distress. She shares with Gwyneth that the event she wishes to address is too painful to speak about or even look at. She tells Gwyneth that she is too afraid and overwhelmed to even address the memory because "it feels like a big issue."

In response to this, Gwyneth helped Rosie gain some much-needed distance from the memory. Gwyneth first tapped with her around the fear of addressing her "big issue." During these rounds of tapping, Rosie used the phrase, "I don't want to open that can of worms." Gwyneth continued to use the metaphor of a "can of worms" to help Rosie gain distance from the overwhelming nature of the event.

When Rosie's fear about addressing the issue subsided some, Gwyneth asked her to describe the can that held the issue, rather than the details of the trauma itself. Rosie described it as a "red, baked-bean-sized, metal can." She shared with Gwyneth that it was located at the very back of the cupboard, in the dark, where she could hardly reach it. Gwyneth asked Rosie to visualize the can of worms in the deepest, darkest corner of her cupboard, using her words and descriptions to tap on the nature and location of the can. She led Rosie in rounds of tapping on "the red can." As they tapped, Rosie volunteered more details about the nature of the can. She told Gwyneth that it was a white can with red writing and was located behind all the things she didn't use very often. As they continued to tap on the visual description of the can, never once mentioning its contents or the details or nature of the trauma, Rosie became visibly calmer.

When Rosie reached a point where she was much more comfortable discussing and tapping about the can, Gwyneth asked her to guess at the intensity of looking at its contents, without opening or looking inside the can. Rosie guessed that the intensity would be an 8. Gwyneth began by leading her in rounds of tapping on the "8 inside the can."

Note how Gwyneth handled the client's fear of addressing the trauma. She did not suggest that Rosie should focus on the details of the issue; in fact, the bulk of the session was spent tapping about the can in the cupboard. Gwyneth never questioned Rosie's judgment or decisions. For many people, addressing an issue via a can inside a cupboard might not seem like a very safe place, but for Rosie, that was a place that represented things getting lost, and it worked for her. As the session continued, Gwyneth continued to help

Rosie address the issue without ever addressing the issue, so to speak. She used the client's language and clues to help her create a safe place to store the issue, focusing the session on safely addressing Rosie's feelings around the can, not the details of the issue that was causing her a great deal of distress.

With any client who is addressing trauma or experiencing symptoms of PTSD, which we will cover in the next chapter, be aware of what you can and cannot handle. Recognize the limits of your ability to work with people, when you may need consultation or to refer the client to another practitioner. Sharing with clients that, because you want the best for them, you need to consult with someone about how to deal with an issue is more of a badge of honor than a mark of failure. If you are willing to admit to clients when you need a little help, you clarify for clients that they are being reasonable when they seek a little help from you.

If you're wondering when you would need to seek consultation, there are certain situations in which it would make sense for you either to refer clients to someone else or to seek consultation for yourself. If a client is presenting with symptoms of extreme emotional distress, recognize that this client might require emergency services that are beyond your skills. Identify, *before you begin seeing clients,* whom you might call in an emergency and what you might do. If you are uncomfortable or unqualified to assist clients in dealing with a particular set of symptoms or trauma, refer them to the appropriate mental health professionals.

For instance, if someone has expressed thoughts of suicide or other forms of self-harm (such as cutting themselves or binge eating and then making themselves vomit) or thoughts of hurting other people, and you are not personally qualified to handle that type of situation, make referrals so these clients can be seen by someone with the experience and expertise to help them. Emergency room personnel are always available to assess clients in an intense emergency.

We firmly believe that EFT can be of significant help to individuals experiencing a wide variety of emotional and physical difficulties. Although it might be tempting to try it on everything, there are professional boundaries, qualifications, and standards that must be respected and enforced for the best interests of the client. In other words, don't go where you don't belong! Create a team with a variety of referral sources to which you can refer when a referral seems necessary, as discussed in the next chapter.

Mental Health Disorders

Nowhere in our use of EFT with various populations does the injunction "Do no harm" apply more than with the population of people with severe mental health diagnoses. There is little research in using EFT with this population.

EFT can be quick and often simple for a phobia or single traumatic event in someone's otherwise supportive world. As Ann says, "EFT can be simple, but people can be very complex." Symptoms of thought disorders, early or ongoing child abuse, a history of not being able to create meaningful relationships, the inability to regulate their emotions, or lack of awareness of what is happening in their body—to name a few challenges—can be complicated to address. Although the process of EFT may be the same once an appropriate and timely specific has been identified, the path to that specific may vary widely.

Throughout this book, we have advocated respecting where clients are at the time they come in and cautiously following their lead. The challenge with this ethical caveat is that it may be difficult and time consuming to truly discover "where" the client is or the depth or severity of their problems.

Some problems have been forgotten, hidden so deeply the client themselves may not remember a problem is there, or they have built such strong "walls" to protect themselves that it takes a great deal of rapport and trust to begin to address it. Though rapport can lead to trust, the two are not the same. The definition of rapport, according to Merriam-Webster, is "a friendly relationship" or "relation marked by harmony, conformity, accord, or affinity." Trust is "belief that someone or something is reliable, good, honest, effective" *(Merriam-Webster)*. In skillful hands, rapport can happen quickly; the client feels that you care. Trust, however, can take significant time, especially with people who have been hurt physically or psychologically, often by those people who "cared."

A key ethical consideration is that of client choice. The right of choice is not simply to use or not to use energy techniques such as EFT. Right of choice needs to be reconsidered every step of the way. It is our job to pay attention to the subtle signs that indicate discomfort or resistance. From a slight frown to moving uncomfortably in the chair, a hesitation or other subtle sign, explore what is happening with your client. The quality of the relationship is a critical factor in the success of a session, as is the timing of any approach.

Timing or readiness is also another ethical consideration. Clients vary widely in their readiness and in their ability and willingness to address and then work to release their traumas.

Starting simply with a deep breathing exercise, calming visualization to relax, or another simple exercise to increase the client's ability to be calm and to recognize what is going on in his or her body can be powerful—and help establish rapport, trust, and a sense of safety.

There are several downsides to going faster than the client is ready to go. First, any "mismatch" of timing or intent creates a loss of rapport; it is to be hoped this will only be temporary, as the practitioner notes the mismatch and is able to recover. In addition, a mismatch can delay the establishment of trust.

Second, the effects of EFT can be so fast that the client may be left in the uncomfortable place of "What happened?" Although this surprise at the quick shift that can occur when using EFT can be a positive experience for the client—and the practitioner—the shift can also be disorienting and the discomfort with the sudden change can increase the client's lack of trust in his or her own perceptions, or may produce enough fear or anxiety that you lose your client.

In the case of thought disorders, this disorientation has the potential for increased disorientation and instability. Further, one EFT practitioner reported a case of a paranoid schizophrenic who became so accepting of his violent urges that he decided he'd take revenge on his boss. Fortunately, the practitioner was able to refer the client to a psychiatrist who responded with the appropriate medication before anything happened.

A third issue to consider in fast perceptual changes of self and the world is the possible upset response of people in the client's life, which might create unexpected problems for the client that he or she does not yet have the skills or emotional strength to deal with in a healthy way. The resistance to change because "it would not be safe for others" is a real factor in some cases. Explore with your client how people in his or her life might respond to this change in the client.

Some clients stop therapy because they are actually getting better and the people on whom they are dependent are reacting to their healthier behavior in ways with which the client was not prepared to deal. Every change has a gain and a loss. Explore the upside and the downside. What other skills or resources does the client need to be able to deal with the changes?

Another ethical consideration is to operate within your scope of practice. It can be counterproductive and, at times, possibly harmful to work with people with more severe problems than your training equips you. Develop referral sources of other professionals and responsibly refer when the problems presented are outside your scope of practice and knowledge. At times, it is possible to work cooperatively with other professionals in a team approach; other times, it may be better to simply refer in a caring manner: "I want the best care for you and these issues are outside of my area."

Later in this chapter, Tracey Middleton provides criteria to consider when thinking of using EFT with someone with a chronic mental disorder. These are excellent guidelines. As Ann is also fond of saying, "Just because we can does not mean we should."

Posttraumatic Stress Disorder

Posttraumatic stress disorder (PTSD) was introduced in the *EFT Level 2 Comprehensive Training Resource*. Sufferers of PTSD experience a stress response in reaction to a traumatic experience that does not go away, or worsens with time. The experience of such stress responses can manifest through persistent reexperiencing of the trauma, such as flashbacks, nightmares, and intense distress at reminders of the event. Clients might also have somatic responses to triggers of the event, including a racing heart, shallow breathing, or possibly an exaggerated startle response. People could experience cognitive and emotional effects, such as numbness, emotional outbursts of anger or irritability, the inability to recall important aspects of the trauma, diminished interest in normal activities, feelings of detachment or estrangement from others, or difficulty thinking about the long-term future. Some clients have symptoms that interfere with daily life, such as increased arousal (hypervigilance such that they need to lock their doors and then check repeatedly to make sure the doors are locked), difficulty falling asleep or staying asleep, altered interest in food, or possibly an avoidance of taking baths or showers or taking many more baths or showers than they used to take in a vain attempt to wash off their bad feelings (National Alliance on Mental Illness [NAMI], 2013).

PTSD has several subcategories:

- Acute Stress Disorder: Responses to the traumatic event occur and, with the help of a support system or treatment, resolve in less than a month.

- PTSD: Responses to the traumatic event interfere with daily functioning and last for months or even years after the event, meeting the diagnostic criteria detailed in the DSM-5.

- Acute PTSD: Responses to the traumatic event last for less than 3 months.

- Chronic PTSD: Responses to the traumatic event last for more than 3 months.

- Delayed-onset PTSD: appears months, and sometimes more than a year, after the initial trauma.

Individuals who have experienced trauma and are suffering from PTSD often have co-occurring conditions (termed "comorbid" conditions). This means that individuals diagnosed with PTSD often experience other, associated conditions at higher rates than people who are not experiencing PTSD. These conditions can include depression, anxiety, sleep disorders, and substance abuse (National Alliance on Mental Illness, 2013). The complexities of PTSD and the high occurrence of associated disorders highlights the importance of thorough professional evaluations for those suffering with symptoms of PTSD, by people who have the training to deal with PTSD, as well as a comprehensive treatment plan designed to address the various aspects of this disorder.

Although EFT can be effective in addressing PTSD, persons experiencing symptoms of PTSD should also see the appropriate medical and mental health professionals whenever necessary. EFT is not designed to replace professional care. It is, instead, a complementary tool that can enhance the level of treatment that people who are living with PTSD are already receiving.

There is an extensive amount of information available on the success of using EFT to address PTSD, including a 2005 study by Swingle and Swingle in which the effects of EFT were observed on car accident victims with symptoms of PTSD. Based on brain-wave data, self-reports, and psychological symptoms, results showed that EFT helped diminish the symptoms of PTSD.

Dr. David Feinstein published a large-scale study in 2004 involving over 5,000 people who had been diagnosed with an anxiety disorder. Participants were randomly divided into two groups: an experimental group (tapping) and a control group (cognitive behavioral therapy and/or medication). Those treated with EFT demonstrated a significantly higher improvement rate, were more often judged as symptom free, and were significantly less likely to experience a relapse or partial relapse in one year's time.

In his 2010 paper, "Rapid Treatment of PTSD: Why Psychological Exposure and Acupoint Tapping May Be Effective," Dr. Feinstein described two randomized controlled trials and six outcome studies with military veterans, disaster survivors, and other individuals who had experienced trauma. He concluded that adding acupoint stimulation to psychological exposure quickly and permanently reduces maladaptive fear responses to traumatic memories and related cues.

Similarly, Dr. Feinstein's 2012 publication in the *Review of General Psychology* critically examined 51 peer-reviewed papers, including 18 randomized controlled trials (RCTs; the Gold Standard of scientific research), on the efficacy of energy modalities for a variety of clinical issues, including chronically traumatized individuals and PTSD. Feinstein reports not only on the efficacy of EFT in studies he evaluated, but also the relatively short treatment time necessary. Clinical trials in his review (including those with veterans, chronically traumatized adolescents, abused adolescents, and several studies comparing the efficacy of EFT with other treatment protocols in previously diagnosed individuals) demonstrated significant reductions of PTSD symptoms and, at times, comorbid conditions such as depression and anxiety (Feinstein, 2012, pp. 6–9).

The research supporting the value of EFT for addressing PTSD continues to grow (see Research.EFTUniverse.com). In addition, there is an increasing body of anecdotal evidence and case stories, some of which appear downright miraculous.

If you decide to work with an individual who is experiencing symptoms of PTSD, you will probably use many of the techniques and approaches detailed in the previous chapter on trauma. Keep in mind that there can be many aspects and manifestations of a complicated disorder such as PTSD. Although EFT can be effective when addressing the symptoms of PTSD, your clients will experience much more profound and lasting success if they address the original trauma(s).

For example, if your PTSD client is having trouble sleeping because of nightmares, address the original trauma first, *if* it is safe for your client to do so. After the original trauma related to the nightmares is addressed in its entirety, the nightmares, which are a symptom of the trauma rather than the whole memory of the trauma, generally resolve easily. Regardless of which tools you use, remember to stress the importance of professional medical and mental health treatment for your client. The psychological safety (and at times the physical safety) of your client is your primary concern.

As a practitioner, your self-care regimen remains an important component to ensure that any negative or triggered reactions you may have are not impacting your relationship with the client. At times, the stories we hear from others may be upsetting to us or trigger issues from our own history. Do what is necessary to address your own reactions, whether through your personal work or a discussion with a mentor on your team, another EFT practitioner, or a therapist.

Depression

For those experiencing depression, it can seem like an insurmountable roadblock, a weight that cannot be lifted. At times, depression may be associated with inexplicably intense emotions that can seem to have no cause, no beginning. Worse still, these intense emotions can appear to the client as *having no end.*

Depression is a relatively common mental disorder characterized by sadness, loss of interest or pleasure in things that used to be interesting or pleasurable, feelings of guilt or low self-worth, disturbed sleep or appetite patterns, tiredness, and poor concentration (Kaplan, Wirtz, Mantel-Teeuwisse, Duthy, & Laing, 2013). Depression can manifest in a variety of ways. It can be long lasting or short-term. It can be continuous, that is, always present, even if to a lesser degree sometimes, or it can be recurrent, which means that it seems to go away for a while but comes back. It can inhibit an individual's ability to function in daily activities, cope with daily life, or maintain interest in hobbies, activities, or relationships. In severe cases, depression can lead to suicide.

Fortunately, EFT offers a potential aid for depression. There is a growing body of research on the use of EFT with depression, including several significant trials that have found when depression is measured before and after EFT, there are often large drops in depressive symptoms (Church, 2013a, p. 4). In working with clients who are experiencing depression, though success is clearly possible, one of the first things to understand is that there are no one-minute wonders. Working with people who have depression often requires dedication, persistence, and patience on the part of both practitioners and clients. Generally, the issues involved with depression take multiple sessions to resolve. There are typically many associated events and beliefs to clear.

According to Dr. Patricia Carrington, one form of depression responds more favorably to straightforward work with EFT than do the other types. She refers to this type of depression as "reactive depression" (Carrington, n.d.). In the DSM-5, reactive depression is labeled an adjustment disorder with depressed mood; it occurs when people have reacted to an event or a series of events with depression, although they were not depressed before the event(s). Since this manifestation of depression is a reaction to something, it has boundaries and, at times, a clear, working path.

A skilled EFT practitioner would have the ability to help clients identify the experiences to which the depression is a reaction. You can then work with your clients to resolve the various aspects of a particular experience or experiences. Some clients will lack a clear memory of the event, and detective work will be necessary to identify the core issue, but once it is discovered, you can apply EFT techniques as you would for any other event. Keep in mind that, although this sounds straightforward, it can still be a long and complicated process, as there is frequently more than one aspect to address. Sometimes you will discover that other events, in addition to the initially identified experience, contributed to a person's depression. You may uncover a series of events or losses. Again, addressing depression can become complex.

Other types of depression can be far more amorphous and enigmatic than the more straightforward reactive depression. These include major depressive disorder and persistent depressive disorder (previously known as dysthymia). These types of depression can seem to have no beginning or end, no clear-cut cause, and no finite bounds to help make them manageable. Dr. Carrington describes these types of depression as having:

> ...roots in the deepest layers of a personality because they are so ingrained, their origins so early in the person's life, and usually they are dim and vague. These depressions have a heaviness about them that makes trying to deal with them by using EFT or by any other means often a test of endurance for the therapist who, time and time again, may bring the person to a place of lightness and feel the weight lift from them—sometimes after they have tapped their way through a whole series of aspects to what seems to be a wonderful result—only to find that at their next appointment the person comes to their session almost as though they had been collapsed and their gains seem to have been swept away. (Carrington, n.d.)

In these situations, the answer is persistence, as long as clients are willing to keep steadfastly working on their issues and are not at high risk of being a danger to themselves or others. The nature of depression causes many depressive clients to have difficulty remaining positive or doing recommended work for themselves between sessions. Dr. Carrington suggests continuing to work with clients, utilizing all of your techniques, tricks, and tools, and remembering to tap for yourself when you feel frustrated or negative (Carrington, n.d.).

In addition to persistently using EFT with clients, remain open to other treatment routes and options. Dr. Carrington recommends exploring allergy and sensitivity testing, if the client is willing and open to it, because dietary and environmental sensitivities or toxicity can play a significant role in the expression of depression symptoms.

Ensure that the client has had a through medical workup, as there could be an underlying physical issue affecting the depression. In chronic cases, discuss with the client the option of a referral to a psychiatric medication specialist or similarly qualified mental health professional. Though energy practitioners rarely consider psychiatric medication as the first option, it can provide the assistance needed for some clients to continue to make progress. Medication can be similar to a cast or a sling for a broken bone; the cast or sling holds the bone in the correct position so the body can heal itself. The cast or sling does not heal anything. Medication is generally not viewed as something that heals mental health issues, but it can contribute to stability while clients heal themselves. EFT can aid the healing process. As Ann Adams has said, "Your client doesn't have to suffer while you are working through their issues."

Please remember that a qualified medical professional will handle all medication-related decisions and changes, including increasing the dosage or discontinuing a medication. Success when addressing depression with EFT does not eliminate the need for a plan and professional supervision when starting or stopping prescribed medication, regardless of how profound the breakthroughs might be when using energy-based treatments such as EFT.

Marina was diagnosed with clinical depression at the age of 17 and had been prescribed a variety of antidepressants over the next 5 years. She had limited success in utilizing both traditional talk therapy and medication. She first sought EFT treatment as an alternative to treatments that appeared to be ineffective. She is now 30. As this book is being written, she is medication free, and the psychiatrist who worked with her throughout her 20s has given her a clean bill of mental health. Her journey from being medicated and depressed to not being medicated and not being depressed was not short and was, at times, extremely difficult. It required persistence, patience, and, frankly, years of EFT sessions with a qualified practitioner.

Marina began the process of EFT treatment while she was still taking antidepressants. She simultaneously worked with her EFT practitioner and maintained an appointment schedule with her counselor and the psychiatrist who managed her medications. That is, she did not quit her participation in conventional medication therapy and talk therapy, but she added EFT sessions to a program of therapy that had previously not been effective for her.

Working extensively with EFT, Marina slowly but surely began to resolve the issues at the heart of her depression. At times, it felt as though for every success there was a relapse, and for every good session there was another day she couldn't get out of bed. Eventually, however, her persistence, and the persistence of her practitioner, paid off. When it was deemed appropriate, her psychiatrist developed a plan with her to progressively reduce all her medication to see if she could do without it. This was another not-so-fast process. She continued to use EFT to address the remaining roots of her depression, as well as for treating setbacks she experienced along the way. She was fortunate to have a network of professionals working with her throughout the process, including a very dedicated, patient EFT practitioner who stuck with her for a long time.

As practitioners, it is important for us to be aware of the attitudes that various professionals have toward EFT, medication, and working as a team. When we refer clients to other professionals, we want to know something about these professionals other than their basic credentials. Marina's psychiatrist and counselor were willing for her to work with an EFT practitioner, whereas some psychiatrists and some therapists would make efforts to dissuade clients from working with alternative health care providers.

Develop a group of other helping professionals willing to work cooperatively with alternative approaches such as EFT. Your goal is to find some of the many caring health care professionals who are willing to work well as a team with you and the client. Nonetheless, clients might come to you for treatment when their psychiatrists or therapists do not approve of energy therapy or alternative therapies. You can offer to have a joint meeting with those other professionals to explain your knowledge and perspective if they are interested in learning more about what you do. Make it clear that you are not suggesting that clients quit seeing their other professionals, because those other professionals have expertise that you do not have. You can sometimes improve people's willingness to be cooperative by offering to do a short explanation or demonstration of EFT treatment. You can refer them to research articles or books. Approaching the initial resistance of other professionals in this way can work well.

In contrast, at times we just have to accept that we are not functioning as part of a cooperative team, but each person who is treating this client is working independently. As noted, depression can be a complex issue and often involves more aspects than most people—even those experiencing it—can imagine. Persistence, patience, and knowing when to seek professional help are key. With these factors in place, success with EFT and depression is possible in most cases.

Other Mental Health Disorders

In addition to depression and PTSD, EFT has been used successfully with other mental health disorders, including anxiety and personality disorders. There is even a growing amount of anecdotal evidence in which EFT has been used to lessen, and in some cases alleviate, symptoms of schizophrenia and schizoaffective disorders; in these cases, however, practitioners focused on one symptom or a small group of symptoms, rather than trying to treat the entire disorder at once.

In one of the many articles on Dr. Patricia Carrington's website, she shares an example from Stairways Behavioral Health in Erie, Pennsylvania, which is a mental health clinic that treats patients with 1) serious mental health diagnoses, and 2) a long history of mental illness. Some of the Stairways professional staff have begun to use EFT with the patient population in conjunction with the standard mental health treatment they provide to patients.

One case from their agency involves a man who had long suffered from a schizoaffective disorder and whose symptoms included "bizarre religious delusions," auditory hallucinations, and blurting out obscenities in public at the prompting of the "voices" he heard (Carrington, 2005–2014). His therapist at the Stairways clinic taught him EFT to help him gain some control over his symptoms, encouraging him to use EFT whenever he heard voices commanding him to do things that he did not want to do.

At the next appointment, the man reported that, although he still heard the voices, using EFT helped him refrain from yelling obscenities in public when the voices told him to. Furthermore, when he used EFT regularly, he heard the voices less frequently. This is an exciting beginning regarding potential uses for EFT as a treatment for serious mental health disorders, including those that involve hallucinations.

This does not mean that all EFT practitioners are being encouraged to use EFT with clients who have psychotic disorders. Practitioners who are doing this work are very experienced EFT practitioners and most have other training in mental health. If you are relatively new to EFT and/or are inexperienced in working with people with more serious mental health disorders (i.e., those who are out of touch with reality at least some of the time), refer these clients to someone who has the experience and the training to deal with such issues.

Clinical social worker Tracey Middleton (www.TappingForPeace.com) has been working in Baltimore, Maryland, with people who have psychotic disorders and dissociative identity disorder (formerly known as multiple personality disorder), and selectively uses EFT with marked benefits. Tracy offers some excellent criteria to determine appropriateness of use with this population.

EFT for Clients with Mental Health Problems

By Tracy Middleton, LCSW-C

It is my responsibility as the therapist to determine if using EFT as an alternative intervention is appropriate and safe for my client and that I have their permission to use it. This can get complicated if my client is experiencing psychotic, delusional, and/or dissociative states. I have developed the following questions to help me discern this:

- Is the client able to develop and articulate clear and concise goals for using EFT? Can the client repeat back to you the goals of EFT as an intervention in order to demonstrate true understanding?

- Is the client able to give informed consent to the use of EFT on those specific issues and goals? Is the client able to understand its benefits, limitations, and possible abreactions? [An abreaction is a strong emotional reaction caused by recalling some memory long repressed. This can be a serious problem with people who have significant challenges in accepting and regulating their emotions.] It is important to get the client's consent at different points in the session while using EFT. They may give consent to start using EFT and in the middle of its application decide to stop. Are you giving the client opportunities to change their mind and reassuring them that it is okay?

- Is there a strong therapeutic alliance already established with the client that could tolerate a new intervention like EFT? Do you know your client well enough to know when a yes to using EFT really means yes? Some clients may say yes to EFT to please you but really don't want to do it. This kind of interaction could lead to harm. Ask open-ended questions thoroughly to determine true consent.

- Have you assessed whether tapping on any of the acupoints might cause a stress response? Show the client a diagram with the EFT acupoints on it and ask which points they would like to use for EFT. Don't assume.

- When using EFT as an intervention for delusions and/or auditory/visual/olfactory hallucinations and/or dissociative states, it is important to assess if the client is competent to consent to their goals and possible benefits. If their goal is to reduce or stop delusions and/or hallucinations, can they verbalize and conceptualize what their life would be like without them? If they are unable to do this, it could increase the likelihood of an abreaction and thus cause possible harm.

- Does the client have enough ego strength to adjust to the cognitive shifts that come with EFT, or could the cognitive shifts cause a decompensation in mental stability? [Note: The term "ego strength" comes from Sigmund Freud's psychoanalytic theory of personality, in which the personality is composed of three elements: the id, the ego, and the superego. Put simply, the id is comprised of primal urges and is present at birth, the superego is comprised of standards and rules acquired from one's parents and society, and the ego is the part of the personality that mediates among the demands and standards of the id, the superego, and reality. "Ego strength" is used to describe individuals who are able to maintain their sense of identity and self in the face of adversity, distress, and conflict and can approach problems with the sense that they can not only overcome, but also grow as a result. Low ego strength refers to individuals who struggle to cope with problems, are overwhelmed by reality, and may avoid challenges and conflict.]

- Have you received permission from your clinical supervisor to use EFT with your client who has severe chronic mental illness and discussed ways to decrease the likelihood of causing harm? Although EFT is an evidence-supported technique, there is limited research regarding its efficacy and limitations in the treatment of delusions, psychosis, hallucinations and/or severe dissociative states.

My experience has taught me that if I can answer yes to the previous questions, then I proceed to use EFT on general and global symptoms. Have the client use EFT on nonthreatening issues *first* to learn how it feels to use the technique and to become familiar with its benefits. Be sure to observe how the client responds to general cognitive shifts. This will give you and the client time to see how EFT is tolerated. This will also allow more time for trust and rapport to develop between you and the client around using EFT. Clients will rely on this until they have trust in EFT.

I had a client who was diagnosed with paranoid schizophrenia. The client was reporting severe distress whenever he walked past his closet because he had a memory (delusion) of being robbed and having all of his belongings stolen from there. The client had been with my agency for many years and it was known that this was one of his delusions and that it had never actually happened. Regardless, it was true for the client and that was all that mattered. After conducting a thorough assessment and obtaining the client's consent, we determined that EFT was an appropriate intervention to try with the client. He was able to articulate what it would be like for him if he no longer feared his closet. The client very much wanted to be able to walk into it again and store his belongings there.

We started by using EFT on how he was feeling in that moment (not related to "The Closet"). I assessed how he tolerated the tapping and its effects. The client seemed to enjoy it and consented to move forward to address "The Closet." We then used EFT to sneak up on the problem. I again assessed how he tolerated the tapping and its effects. The client gave consent again to continue. The client was unable to guess how intense it would be if he only thought about "The Closet," as preparation for the Tearless Trauma Technique. Instead, he went directly into the stress response about the issue. Our rapport was already established at this point, and I was able to lead the client through EFT in a gentle way and at his pace.

After about 15 more minutes of tapping on different aspects and reassessing for consent and symptoms, the client walked up to his closet, opened the door, and walked in! He immediately started crying and yelling to me how good it felt to be in his closet. He had a huge smile and tears running down his face.

I had another client with paranoid schizophrenia who wanted to use EFT on his voices. After in-depth exploration through the previous questions, the client was able to develop clarity around his goal by saying, "I don't want my voices to go away. I just want them to quiet down. They are my friends and I don't want them to leave." This was critical information for me to know and if I had rushed ahead with EFT without a thorough exploration of his goal, I could have missed hearing it. His stated goal made me apprehensive about using EFT because I was concerned that his voices might go away and that this might cause him harm. As I could not guarantee that EFT would not make his voices go away, I discerned that EFT was not an appropriate intervention to use with this client.

I have also used EFT to treat dissociative identity disorder. It takes great skill to map each alter to determine the answers to all of the assessment questions for them and the host. [In terms of dissociative identity disorder, *alter* refers to dissociated states of identity. The difference between identities can be "distinct and dramatic" (Putnam, 1989) and can be observed in speech, mannerisms, sense of history, sense of body, and so on. Multiple personality states, dissociated or not, cannot be present at the same time but can switch rapidly. Herman (2012) states, "Those with dissociative identity disorder tend to switch when there is a perceived psychological threat. The switching allows a distressed state to retreat, while a state who is more competent will handle the emerging situation."]

Some alters may have more ego strength than others, and I have seen where the host is the only one who consents to use EFT. Some alters may consent to using EFT, while others may not. When assessed appropriately for a specific alter and/or host, I use EFT to help develop safe places. I also find that it works great in treating specific trauma that each alter is holding and that it can facilitate an alliance between alters and host for working toward the goal of integration. This is a very complicated process since there are multiple ego states to assess for in terms of consent, therapeutic alliance, strengths, and possible abreactions. You must explore enough in the interview to assess how cognitive shifts could affect the host and affect the alters' relationships to each other. In these cases, I am assessing for risk and determining the use of EFT throughout the process on each given day.

Using EFT with people who have been diagnosed with severe and chronic mental illness entails a different level of exploration and assessment than when working with clients who have relatively simple and straightforward issues. It requires flexibility and persistence in assessing risk. Client consent needs to be determined throughout the process. Among other things, practitioners need to encourage their clients verbally to be consistently true to themselves, which could, at some point, result in clients deciding to discontinue using EFT. This is particularly important when working with clients who have poor ego strength. We certainly do not want to encourage clients to remain focused on their treatment to please us when they would rather take a break.

Although reports such as those from Dr. Carrington and Tracy Middleton are promising for the use of EFT with serious mental health disorders, reading Tracy's list of assessment questions reinforces the fact that you must exercise caution when working with clients who have complicated issues and mental health problems. Particularly in these cases, EFT should be used as a supplement to professional mental health treatment, and it is incredibly important that these clients maintain their relationship with the appropriate mental health professional.

There are currently an insufficient number of clinical reports and no published research on using EFT with diagnosable thought disorders and how such clients would react to using EFT. Clients with these issues are best referred to mental health professionals with specialized training. The Hippocratic Oath of "Do no harm" and the caveat "Don't go where you don't belong" both particularly apply here. Though EFT might or might not be helpful with these types of disorders and symptoms, be aware that these individuals are often in need of consistent, professional treatment, might be taking a variety of medications, and often suffer from hallucinations and delusions. Again, EFT is not intended to replace professional medical treatments and interventions.

The body of evidence for the efficacy of EFT in the treatment of mental health problems such as PSTD, phobias, anxiety, and depression is growing, but you may or may not be qualified to work with persons suffering from serious mental health disorders. There are EFT practitioners who have clinical backgrounds and experience in this area, or who are comfortable working closely with a client's clinician or therapist. If you do not have this type of experience and training, even if you believe you are ready to work with complicated clients, you must be prepared to refer them to someone who is licensed and qualified to work with people who have these disorders.

Referrals

Referrals are an important part of your EFT practice. Having access to a network of professionals (both EFT and otherwise) to whom you can refer is useful and can be necessary when you encounter clients with whom you are uncomfortable working, who present with symptoms or complaints outside of your experience or skill level, or who may need treatment outside of EFT. As an EFT practitioner, it is your ethical and moral responsibility to make these connections and build this network as a resource for both your clients and you.

Many times, relationships with other EFT professionals to whom you may be able to refer clients will be formed during your training as an EFT practitioner. That is, EFT classes, trainings, and workshops often put you in a position to network with other EFT practitioners, who might have a specialty, education, background, and experience different from yours, or have other valuable insights and skills that could be helpful to you in your practice. These educational environments will also put you in contact with a qualified trainer who may be able to provide insight, be a mentor, be someone to whom you can refer specific clients, or play another important role in your professional network.

Karin has built a network of professionals and resources over the years. As a professional courtesy, she offers to pay for any consultation. Her network includes:

- A psychologist who uses various modes of energy psychology in practice
- A former administrator of a mental health facility who has studied EFT
- A past president of the American Association of Psychotherapists
- A licensed clinical social worker specializing in work with teenagers
- A psychiatrist
- A family therapist
- At least one experienced person in every complementary modality she uses in her practice
- A specialist working with serious diseases and pain
- A nurse practitioner
- A medical doctor
- Various colleagues she met through trainings, workshops, and Internet searches who have experience in a particular specialty.

Karin has an additional list that she uses in circumstances in which she believes a client is best assisted by working with an EFT professional with a certain specialty.

In addition to the individuals you meet during EFT workshops, classes, and trainings you attend throughout your career, there are a variety of online networks you can use to find individuals to whom you can refer the clients you need to refer.

Become familiar as well with the various resources available in your community. Referrals can work both ways. Building relationships with local practitioners, including medical doctors, chiropractors, mental health professionals, and others who might refer clients to you will often be beneficial to you. Physicians who are aware of the benefits of other types of therapy sometimes want help for their patients who appear to be insufficiently responsive to medication. Dr. Sherrod has worked with clients who were referred by their physicians as a result of their intransigent high blood pressure. Putting the time and effort into establishing and building these relationships can provide you with resources for referrals you may need to provide clients in the future and also result in new business for your practice.

When Kari discovered that several of the clients she was seeing were patients at a local chiropractic office where acupuncture services were also offered, she took the opportunity to reach out to the doctor there and explain what she did and her connection with several of his clients. The resulting relationship has not only benefitted her existing clients in that she is now able to suggest a reliable, professional chiropractic practice to her clients who might benefit from chiropractic care, but the chiropractor also suggests her services to some of his chronic patients who are afraid of the needles used in traditional acupuncture.

Forming a network for referrals often requires that you reach out to the professionals in your community and cultivate connections with them.

Allergies and Sensitivities

According to the American Academy of Allergy, Asthma and Immunology (AAAAI), up to 30% of the worldwide population suffers from some form of allergic rhinitis (seasonal allergies, hay fever, etc.), up to 10% of the world's population suffers from drug and antibiotic allergies, more than 8% of children and 8.5% of adolescents and adults suffer from multiple food allergies, and the "rise in prevalence of allergic diseases has continued…for more than 50 years" (AAAAI, 2013). Allergies and sensitivities affect millions of people a year.

As these statistics indicate, the chances of EFT practitioners being presented with a client having an allergic reaction or an immune system disorder are significant. EFT is a useful tool for addressing allergies and sensitivities, from hay fever to animal or pet dander allergies to food sensitivities and seasonal allergies.

Using EFT with Allergies

Addressing allergies with EFT can sometimes be as simple as working with the physical symptoms of the reaction. For example, if clients are suffering from seasonal allergies or hay fever, tapping on their specific symptoms (e.g., stuffy nose, sinus pain, pressure, etc.) can bring some level of relief. Nonetheless, it would be more likely that the issue of allergies will be one that requires a holistic approach because the involved issues tend to be layered and can be much more complex than "even though I have this stuffy nose."

We recommend a holistic approach for allergies and sensitivities because, in addition to addressing the physical symptoms and manifestation of the allergy, which are important aspects of an allergy-sufferer's treatment, you will want to find and address the root cause(s) of the allergies. This can be environmental, which means that you might need to address the aspects around what clients identify as their triggers, which could be emotional. Generally, you will need to find and address the symptoms, environmental issues, and any involved events and emotions.

The first step in addressing clients suffering from allergies is to take a detailed history. Taking clients' history is always important, whatever the presenting problem. When working with allergies, pay attention to information including:

- When did the allergies begin?

- When do the symptoms occur? A particular time of day or a particular day of the week? Do they vary by seasons? Do they occur before social events? After social events?

- Where do they occur? Home? Office? Stores? Outside? Hospitals? Doctors' offices?

- What seem to be the triggers for allergic reactions?

- What significant events were occurring in the client's life at the onset of the allergies, or even a few months before?

- Is there a family history of allergies? Are there family beliefs about allergies? (For example, "You can't do anything about allergies; you just have to put up with them.")

- Is there a memory or trauma related to the substance to which the client is allergic?

This type of detailed information about clients, their histories, and their allergic disease or sensitivity will function as the beginning of your detective work as a practitioner. It also lays the groundwork for you to help clients address their allergies and sensitivities in a thorough and holistic way, making sure to resolve as many aspects related to the allergies as possible.

Sometimes, clients who are suffering from allergies will remember a trauma or significant event that occurred around or slightly before the onset of the allergies. For example, client Madeline suffered from an allergy to hydrangeas, a flower common in the spring and summer where she lives. When asked to think about what was happening in her life at the time she remembers the allergy beginning, it occurred to her that her first husband used to bring her hydrangeas. She found out later in their marriage that he did so only after he had seen his mistress; his infidelity would later be at the root of their painful divorce.

In situations like this, the trauma can be addressed with EFT. Once all the aspects of the traumatic memory are cleared, and you have tested for other, related events or aspects, the allergy symptoms may well disappear. Sometimes, additional tapping is needed for the actual symptoms and the emotions associated with the symptoms (e.g., frustration at not being able to breathe, annoyance at coughing, etc.) in order for the issue to clear entirely.

Client Tom had an allergy to cats for as long as he could remember. He also remembered that his mother, who worked evenings, would leave him as a small child at his grandmother's house while she worked. His grandmother had a couple of ill-tempered cats. Certainly, his feelings about being left by his mother needed to be addressed, but he was also scratched by the cats on several occasions, without acknowledgment of the problem or support from his grandmother. Tom didn't remember if that is when his allergies began. But exploring the memories he presented around being left with his grandmother and no support around the cat scratches made these memories a fertile place to explore.

After addressing memories with EFT, testing for the many aspects as you work through the stories, and checking the presenting symptoms again, you may discover that more exploration will be necessary to identify and resolve additional events or memories.

If there is a family history of a specific allergy—or a family history of any disease, for that matter—the issue might not lie with the client alone. Especially if clients believe their allergies were passed down to them from another relative, it might be effective to address this directly with EFT, before exploring the possible triggers in the client's own life.

For example, Julian shared on his intake form that he believed he had an allergy to milk because it was passed down to him by both his father and his grandfather. Whether or not this is true is unimportant; it is what the client believes, and therefore it is significant. This generational aspect could be treated as just that—an aspect of the larger issue. Tap around clients' beliefs that their allergies came from another family member, tap around any emotions or frustrations related to those beliefs, and clear the aspect(s) related to inheriting an allergy before moving onto additional aspects of the larger issue. This may require some exploring.

Peeling the Layers

Working with and resolving allergies and sensitivities will likely require peeling away layers and ensuring that multiple aspects have been addressed, tested, and resolved before the allergy itself will be resolved. If a client comes to you with an allergy, but no obvious root cause, there are other approaches you can try. One of these we addressed earlier in the book: make it up (the "Let's Pretend" Technique). You can have clients make up a plausible and feasible story that could be related to their allergies and approach it as if it were real.

A second approach involves the substance that triggers the allergy. So, for example, if clients have an allergy to cat hair or dairy products, you could place some cat hair or piece of cheese in a glass, metal, or ceramic container, have clients hold the container in their lap, and tap on the "stuff" in the jar. You don't have to know exactly how the allergen is affecting clients for this to bring some relief. Clients can hold or touch the container while they tap on their body's reaction to it, as they ask their body to release their sensitivity to the particular substance. Example: "Even though my body is reacting to ____, I accept myself and my body and ask my body to release its sensitivity to ____." This exercise alone might bring relief, or it might bring up more information for the person tapping. Either is great!

Case Study: Bee Sting Allergy

Early in Ann's journey into EFT, she "experimented" on her friends. For example, "Joree" wanted to work on her bee sting allergy. She took an annual shot to prevent her from having an intense reaction to bee venom. Joree lived on the outskirts of town with lots of open fields, flowers, and woods. She very much wanted to be free of the allergic (and dangerous) reaction if she should be stung. Her next test and next shot were 11 months in the future.

Ann discussed in some depth with Joree that there was no proof that the energy work would resolve her allergy. (Ethically, practitioners should not promise any specific outcome. As practitioners, we teach clients to tap on meridian points and we encourage them to continue their work at home between sessions, but we do not have responsibility for what this work will accomplish.)

Joree said she would continue her medication and all cautions in addition to coming to EFT sessions. Her goal was to see if the annual blood test for the allergy-causing antibodies would prove negative. They began using EFT with incidents in Joree's life around the time she was stung and first had symptoms. These led, as EFT often does, to earlier similar events and emotions. They tapped on symptoms and emotions around taking the shots and fears associated with the problem. After several sessions, they exhausted everything Joree felt was relevant.

Joree and Ann had been friends for years, and as often happens when using EFT with friends and relatives, Joree did not want Ann going further into all her "stuff." As we have emphasized throughout this book, how far clients (or in this case, a friend) want to go is their choice. Getting into personal issues with friends and family members shifts relationships. It is not possible to predict how relationships might shift. Traditional therapists are expected to let their friends and family members seek therapy from other people, and generally do not provide therapy for people with whom they have personal relationships.

EFT practitioners do tend to work with friends and family members, but it remains wise to be careful about doing this. Many personal friends and family members are not willing to go deeply into their issues with a practitioner whom they know well. They could become uncomfortable being around someone who "knows too much about them."

So when Joree said, "I can't think of anything else to address," Ann respected her position that she had done enough. Joree then shifted the conversation to Ann's recent training in NLP. So, in addition to using EFT techniques, Ann showed her the NLP process for allergies. As Joree left that session, she said she would use EFT every day for her anxiety around the allergy to bees before she went outside.

Ann and Joree did not discuss her allergy again or do more EFT together. Joree called excitedly 11 months later that she had "passed the test!" and did not have to take the shots anymore. She said she had religiously continued to use EFT and the NLP visualization daily on her own. Joree was elated by the results.

Many clients are less motivated and consistent than Joree. Her case brings up interesting speculations. Would EFT work every time if clients were that consistent? Was Joree consistent in doing the work because she was experiencing positive effects? Would EFT have worked alone? The parameters within which EFT works on allergies are unknown. Though, again, one should never promise a positive outcome, some practitioners are certainly using EFT successfully for many clients with allergies.

Gathering Information Is Key

Addressing allergies and sensitivities with EFT is worth trying. Although it might not always resolve the allergy, sometimes, while working on allergies or sensitivities, other issues come to clients' attention. Addressing seemingly unrelated events involving emotional reactions or uncomfortable memories can sometimes lead to allergy relief for clients.

The key to working with clients who have allergies and sensitivities is gathering enough information, both in sessions and in a thorough client history. Discovering these details provides the path to peeling away the aspects and layers involved in the client's allergies. Persistence pays off when it comes to allergies and sensitivities¬, as it often does with other issues. A specific sensitivity might need to be revisited and retested multiple times during the process.

It is also important to note that some allergic reactions (like Joree's) can be dangerous. Always err on the side of caution when it comes to your clients and their health. Testing in vivo (i.e., in real life situations) is often a very useful EFT method, but if a potential allergic reaction is life threatening or potentially harmful to a client's well-being, direct confrontation with the substance is not best and, in fact, is contraindicated.

Note in Joree's case that Ann made no attempt to test the bee sting reaction, and indeed cautioned her against directly creating a challenge to her system regarding an allergic response. Testing was, however, conducted for the aspects of each related event, emotion, and physical sensation Joree presented. The ultimate test, which was the blood test for antibodies in reaction to bee venom, was conducted by a medical professional and did not put Joree's life at risk.

Working with Parts

There are a variety of therapeutic approaches that utilize the concept of "parts," including Inner Family Systems Therapy (IFS), Dialectical Behavior Therapy (DBT), and several schools of psychodynamic therapy. Similarly, the concept of parts can be integrated into EFT. For example, when clients are struggling with conflicting beliefs or when they show signs of internal conflict, one part of them is struggling with another part of them. In EFT, the term "parts" refers to any opposing or conflicting beliefs, attitudes, emotions, positions, or inclinations that exist within one person.

When using EFT with clients who are experiencing an internal conflict or struggling with conflicting beliefs, it is often helpful to recognize the parts of that conflict in your EFT language. For example, Kari recently worked with a client who was struggling to quit smoking. The woman, whom we will call Casey, wanted very much to stop smoking, and had already initiated the process of quitting before coming to see Kari.

Casey shared with Kari that she didn't like smoking most of the time, but when she was at parties or at a bar, she believed she needed to smoke to be comfortable. As Casey was using language such as "Part of me hates smoking, but another part of me needs to smoke when I'm with a big group of people," Kari incorporated the language into their tapping rounds, recognizing and appreciating the two conflicting parts of Casey. This can be as simple as: "Even though I really want to quit smoking, there is a part of me that still needs to smoke when I'm at a party, and I truly and deeply accept both parts anyway," or "Even though one part of me wants to quit smoking, and another part doesn't, I truly and deeply accept myself anyway, including the part that still needs to smoke."

Many times, you can help clients move forward by helping them recognize and be respectful toward the conflicting parts or beliefs they are experiencing. In Casey's case, recognizing and accepting that there was a part of her that experienced a strong desire to smoke, and understanding that it didn't take away from the other part of her that wanted to quit smoking, helped her recognize that the part of her that still felt compelled to smoke was a legitimate part of her. Casey did eventually quit smoking, and she reports that acknowledging all of her—even the parts that wanted to smoke and the reasons they felt compelled to do so—empowered her to find new solutions that didn't involve cigarettes.

Clients may want to "get rid of" a particular behavior, attitude, bad habit, or something else. They often discover to their dismay, however, that the harder they fight against a part of themselves, the harder it is to make that part go away. Rather than striving to get rid of a part, it is more effective to honor and appreciate why we developed that part in the first place. All of us, clients and practitioners alike, had good reasons for developing some strategies and beliefs for dealing with life's challenges that we no longer want to keep following because they no longer work for us. Sometimes, frankly, our previous strategies for solving problems and our previous belief systems have become serious problems themselves.

Instead of having clients focus on what's wrong with the parts of them that have now become problematic, clients benefit from learning to be open to themselves and to their previous need to develop those strategies and beliefs, given the situations they were in when they developed those approaches and ideas. When clients compassionately notice the needs they had that they were addressing by developing those strategies and beliefs, rather than disrespecting themselves for having developed those strategies and beliefs or rejecting those strategies and beliefs, clients more quickly give themselves permission to find more effective ways to solve problems and deal with life's challenges. Arnold Beisser (1971) noticed and wrote about what he called a paradoxical theory of change, which is that when people accept themselves as they are right now, rather than trying to be something they're not, they are actually more likely to make the changes they want to make.

Even if clients are highly motivated to make changes, they also are likely to have some reservations about changing. Any change means giving up or losing something. If there was no benefit to a particular behavior, thought, or belief, we would have already given it up. Finding, accepting, and addressing the "part" that holds the benefit is often what resolves the conflict and allows clients to move forward. Most of the decisions we face in life represent a conflict of pros and cons, challenges of "parts" that want to do one thing and "parts" that want to do something else. This internal back and forth is a normal part of everyday life. When faced with decisions, changes, and new things, we all have "parts." Discover, address, and appreciate all of the "parts" that come up for your clients.

Visualization

Visualizing the different parts can help. Many EFT practitioners regularly use "parts" visualization techniques in their practices with great success. If your clients are open to it, you can invite them to visualize and describe their parts. There are no limits as to what their parts can be or look like; that is entirely open to client interpretation. Some clients will envision a shape or object. Encourage as much detail as possible, asking questions about what their part or parts look like. For example, Casey could have described the part of her that wanted to smoke as a "black lump in my gut," and in that case, Kari would have tapped with her using that language and description.

For some clients, it may help to invite them to take their parts out and place those parts in front of them. This can offer clients an opportunity to experience the degree of separation they need to visualize more clearly. In an example like this, Casey could have taken both conflicting parts concerning smoking and placed them on the table in front of her. An ashtray, a scared little girl, or any imagery that came to mind could have represented the part of her that wanted to smoke. On the other hand, an angel, a shiny glowing light, or a confident picture of herself could have represented the part of her that didn't want to smoke. Any imagery is acceptable.

Either method of identifying the parts works; it all depends on what feels more comfortable to your clients. As always, take your cues from clients, use their descriptors and language, and encourage them to notice details about their parts through responding to your questions.

Note that your questions could encourage clients to better visualize their parts whether they agree that your questions are on the mark or they respond by saying that your questions are off the mark. For example, you could ask clients questions about the black lump in their gut, perhaps asking if the lump has always been the same size or has changed in size. Clients could respond by saying, "It's not the size that's important; it's how heavy it is" or "Now that you mention it, it seems to have gotten bigger recently" or "I can't tell what size it is because it's buried in my gut and I can't get a good view of it even when I try to put it in front of me." Whatever way clients answer your questions provides helpful information.

Case Study:
The Parts in Chronic Back Pain

A client with chronic back pain told Karin that nothing she had ever tried had helped, and tapping wouldn't help either. Karin responded, "Then you have nothing to lose, right? I'd like to try something." She asked the woman to close her eyes and pretend that the pain in her back was an object. (This is similar to the technique described in the Level 2 book called "Color of Pain.")

The woman laughed and said, "You won't believe it...It's Sponge Bob Square Pants. He's in my left lower back, but I have pain on both sides." Karin asked her to look at the right side as well. The client said, "I don't see anything...oh wait, it's hiding. It's a long red balloon-looking thing. It's got eyes but no arms or legs—this is crazy."

Karin then asked her to take the two objects out of her back and pretend to set them in front of her, one on each knee. She instructed the client to tap around her points while she imagined listening to the two objects talk to each other. Instead, the client stopped abruptly and almost gave up because she felt strange doing this technique. Karin paused and tapped, saying, "Even though this is crazy, I'll pretty much do anything to get rid of this pain, even talk to an imaginary Sponge Bob and a red balloon." After a few rounds, the client laughed at how ridiculous it all seemed and went back to listening to Sponge Bob Square Pants and the red balloon talk to each other while sitting on her knees.

The story became very elaborate. Sponge Bob hated Red Balloon because Sponge Bob loved to play and Red Balloon hated to play. Red Balloon, on the other hand, hated Sponge Bob because he never did any work, and Red Balloon felt it had to do everything. As the story went on, Sponge Bob invited Red Balloon to a playground, and although Red Balloon didn't have time to play, it agreed to take 5 minutes, but only if Sponge Bob promised to do some work at least once. On the playground, they first went to a slide; however, Red Balloon couldn't climb up the ladder without arms and legs. Sponge Bob offered to carry him up. Red Balloon insisted that he was too heavy, but Sponge Bob said he would work really hard so that Red Balloon could finally have some fun. Red Balloon squealed with happiness as it slid down the slide.

When it was Sponge Bob's turn to go down the slide, he was afraid he would hurt himself. Red Balloon said, "I'll stay here and you can land on me, I'm soft." This newfound partnership continued to a small lake by the playground where there were paddleboats. Of course, Red Balloon had no legs, so Sponge Bob offered to pedal so that Red Balloon could enjoy the boat ride.

Karin reminded the client to continue tapping while telling this story. After a while, it was time to leave the playground, but Sponge Bob didn't want to go. Karin asked if the client would be willing to put the playground in her back with Sponge Bob and Red Balloon so they could play now and then. This made everyone very happy. Red Balloon shared how proud and grateful it was to Sponge Bob for helping it, and Sponge Bob was so happy that Red Balloon would finally play with him.

Karin asked the client how her back was feeling. The client was shocked that she no longer felt any pain. She expressed her doubt that she would remain pain free. Karin suggested that she allow Sponge Bob and Red Balloon to play on the playground anytime her back hurt. The client contacted Karin a few weeks later to report that the pain did return, but it wasn't nearly as bad as it had been. She also shared that she had actually tried the "playground trick" again and, much to her surprise, it had worked. She laughed, "I'd much rather have a playground with Sponge Bob and Red Balloon than pain."

Identify the Parts as People

Another, more literal method for identifying and working with parts is demonstrated in an article by psychotherapist and EFT practitioner Masha Bennett (2011) who often uses parts work in her EFT practice. When she senses that a client is struggling with an internal conflict, or the client uses language that indicates that parts may be a viable option for the session, she asks the client to identify the parts as people. She asks questions like:

- If the part of you that is responsible for [the undesired behavior or negative feeling] were a person, what would it look like?
- Is it male or female?
- What is he or she wearing?
- How old is he or she?
- Does he or she have a name? What would you call him or her?

In this case, the character that the client creates or describes functions as a metaphor for the part in question. Bennett taps with her clients to acknowledge the part, using the client's description and language as a guide. She tracks progress through the appearance of the person or character the client created. After the client has gained a level of acceptance concerning the existence of the part, she asks, "If this part were trying to help in some way, what might its purpose be?" (Bennett, 2011). She then uses the language offered by the client regarding the potential positive intention of the part during her rounds of tapping. For example, in the case about trying to quit smoking, Casey might have said, "Even though I don't like this part of me, I recognize that it is only trying to make me feel comfortable and accepted when I'm in a large group."

Many times, acknowledging the existence of the part and recognizing the positive thing it is seeking to accomplish (which could have to do with safety, love, strength, etc.) can help clients make dramatic changes. You might encourage clients to develop alternative methods to detect the positive intentions of the undesired part, or assign the undesired part an alternative job. That is, sometimes the undesired parts do not need to go away, but they function effectively if they undergo some changes. As always, take your cues from clients regarding what works best.

Bennett also suggests that, if there is a conflict present, it might be necessary for the client to create a visual image of the opposing part, tapping to integrate the two parts. For example, Casey could have created an image of an insecure teenage girl to represent the part of her that still felt compelled to smoke in social situations. To represent the part of her that does not want to smoke, she could create an image of a happy, healthy, confident version of herself. If it's helpful, you can ask the client to draw pictures of the two conflicting parts.

Bennett suggests then asking questions about the opposing parts, such as:

- How far away from each other are they?

- What are their facial expressions?
- What do they feel about each other?
- What do they want from each other?

All of these questions and visualizations provide valuable information on which you and the client can tap. Your role is to remain neutral and nonjudgmental about the imagery and words the client uses, continuing to ask questions to gauge how the imagery is changing as you tap. If you chose to have clients draw images to represent their opposing parts, they might make changes or adjustments to the images as their parts change. The parts might move closer to one another. They might change in their ages, expressions, or appearance. Feelings and emotions that were not previously felt might begin to be present.

As the process continues, clients might create an image in which the two opposing parts make a gesture of togetherness, such as hugging or otherwise accepting each other. Bennett (2011) writes:

> The details of these transformations are utterly unique to each individual and the length of time that true integration may take can vary widely...
> In addition to the healing properties of EFT, this is the most important component of healing these internal wars that are such a common part of the process of human change, development, and transformation.

As always, take your cues from the client. Do not force integration if the client is not ready. Don't be afraid to end sessions without the parts being fully integrated. Integration can take several sessions. Tap on whatever information arises, allowing the integration process to be client led, which means that it will happen naturally and organically.

Kathryn Sherrod, PhD, shared a story with Karin about a client whom we will call Jennie:

> Jennie came for treatment because she had developed PTSD and panic attacks that resulted from being assaulted at work. Simplifying Jennie's situation slightly, we can say that one part of her wanted to go back to viewing the world as a positive place so she could quit worrying about ever being hit again, while the other part of her wanted to remain permanently on guard, so she would never be vulnerable to being hit again. Notice that both parts were working toward the same goal (i.e., not being hit again); they just had opposing ideas regarding how to attain that goal.
>
> After tapping, Jennie resolved her dilemma of having opposing parts by recognizing that it made sense for her to be a bit more wary about people than she had been in the past, in order to keep herself safe enough to recognize and benefit from being open to the positive people in the world.
>
> A distorted belief that Jennie thought was true when she first came to EFT sessions was, "You get back what you give people." Jennie gave people her best. She was consistently considerate. She finally realized that being

nice to people invites them to be nice back, and increases the probability that they will be nice back, but it does not guarantee that they will be nice back. She learned that how we treat people affects the probabilities regarding the ways in which they respond to us, but other people have free will and they can choose to respond to us in a different way than the way we treated them. (Personal correspondence, 2014)

Working with parts can provide a powerful tool for clients who are dealing with internal conflicts. It offers ways to gather information about the client's struggle. Remember that every exercise, visualization, and round of tapping in an EFT practice is a way of gathering more information for the next steps. In other words, you don't need to be concerned about knowing the right words, the right answers, or even knowing how to reconcile two opposing parts. The information you need comes from clients. Whatever clients say is exactly that—more information. Your goal is to facilitate the process, regardless of how it takes shape within the session.

Excellence in EFT

There is no question that we are all still learning, still walking the path of becoming a better practitioner and person. Part of your journey in EFT is being consistently open to learning and becoming aware of the elements of your profession, your practice, and your passion in which you can strive for excellence. When we say "excellence," we do not mean perfection. Perfection is a standard that is unattainable because we are all human. What we do mean is engaging in a continual process to improve yourself and your work, developing your practice, engaging in ongoing learning, and moving forward in the journey to become the best practitioner you can be. This chapter addresses some of the topics we, the authors, believe are important in this journey. We hope it will provide food for thought in your own quest for excellence.

Regard for Client Safety

Throughout the EFT process, clients can dredge up intense emotional issues. As practitioners, with experience, you will be in tune with clients so you can address these reactions. Always tread lightly when clients seem to be approaching intense issues. Remember to use distancing techniques when necessary. Never force or even encourage clients to go where they aren't ready to go. Despite the existence of "one-minute wonders," this is not a race to the finish. Clients need to feel safe exploring issues and emotions at their own pace.

With practice and experience, you might start to sense when clients are becoming uncomfortable and might want to slow the pace or take a break. Calling attention to what you are noticing can be helpful, using questions and comments such as: What just happened? I felt a shift in energy just then. What did you notice in your body while we did that last round? What are you experiencing right now?

There are many levels of highly emotional responses. The most intense of these are often referred to as abreactions. Whenever clients display signs of intense emotion, which can include but are not limited to tears, change in skin color, anger, stammering, inability to communicate, and rapid breathing, first and foremost, keep tapping. (Note that the appearance of any of these symptoms does not necessarily indicate an abreaction. Your clients may cry or respond emotionally throughout a session for a variety of reasons. It is the remarkably high intensity of the reaction that denotes a true abreaction.)

You don't have to use any words. When emotions are running high, it is usually best to tap with or on clients (if you have permission and it is safe to do so) until they have cleared enough of the emotion that they can continue. You might say something comforting such as "You are safe here with me" or "Stay with me." Encourage them to keep their eyes open.

Techniques that help clients remain in the present are called grounding techniques. The intention in using EFT is to keep the person in the present time, with the feelings they have of the past focused on how such feelings are manifesting *in the present time*. If your clients seem lost in the memory or emotion, take steps to bring them back to the present. Ask them to describe the room where they are sitting or what they had for breakfast. Ask them to press on their wrists, look in your eyes, take their shoes off and feel the floor under their feet, or anything that helps keep them connecting to themselves, to you, and to the here and now.

Helping your client stay present in these moments is key to moving with them through the abreaction. Above all else, stay calm. If you remain calm, not only will you be better able to navigate the intense situation, but it will also help clients move through their emotion, rather than getting lost in it.

Experiencing an abreaction with a client can be challenging, or even frightening, but EFT is an effective tool for working through high levels of emotion. It is often effective to simply stay calm, keep tapping, and use encouraging, soothing words to help the client stay in the present time with you. After the emotional intensity has subsided, you can decide if it is safe for your client to continue. If a client's emotions do not subside, or if you think a client might be a danger to him or herself, contact the appropriate medical professionals.

Why, in this case, did we say you could decide if it is safe for your client to continue rather than allowing your client to make that decision? Sometimes clients get so lost in their emotions that they are overwhelmed. They are not thinking clearly. They might be too confused and too upset to make good decisions. If that were to happen, you need to make sure your client is taken care of by someone. You might call a friend, a family member, or emergency services, or failing all of those approaches, you might decide to take your client to an emergency room if you don't believe your client can get there independently. Although we are mentioning ways to deal with such intense reactions, having clients become this overwhelmed by emotion is a rare occurrence. Assisting clients in moving through their traumatic experiences at their own pace helps to avoid abreactions.

Rapport

Developing solid rapport is an essential component to the efficacy of your EFT practice and the safety of your clients. Rapport refers to the empathetic connection you build with clients that allows them to feel safe and comfortable sharing personal information, trust you during the EFT process, and be more open to exploring their emotions and feelings. Rapport with traumatized and/or abused clients can be slow to build. Sometimes, clients who are highly vulnerable might react to something you said or did as if you have broken trust with them. If that happens, you can apologize and explain that you did not intend for them to feel distress at what you said or did. As a way to rebuild trust, it may be helpful to ask what they would have preferred you to say or do.

Some ways that you can build rapport with your clients include:

- Present yourself and your practice in a professional manner that establishes a sense of safety and credibility.

- Clarify their expectations about coming to see you. What are they expecting to happen?

- Clarify their readiness to change. Not everyone comes in ready to change their situation. Some need to just discuss their situation and explore pros and cons.

- Answer questions and address any concerns or confusions about EFT, especially for clients who have no experience with the modality.

- Explain how you work with EFT. Preframe what to expect in an EFT session and how you will help clients locate a specific event. Explain that you will assist them as they work through each detail of the story. Share with them that "the strength of EFT is in addressing the specific events" in their story and that you will be stopping them along the way to make sure you address all the details of the story. Explain that the goal of EFT is to address issues as painlessly as possible and you may also stop them to back out and go more slowly where there are intense emotions.

- Take the time to truly listen to your clients. Many of us want to jump right into tapping at the first indication of a specific. Allowing clients to feel fully heard can be invaluable to their progress. Helping clients realize that you respect how they are working through their issues in the very best way they can contributes to your ability to help them resolve their frustrations regarding their view of self, their view of others, and whether the world in general is benign, loving, or intentionally challenging.

- In sessions, maintain personal space boundaries that are comfortable for both you and clients. Always ask permission if you would like to tap on a client or try something new or unexpected.

- Hold sessions in a space that is professional, comfortable, and private for your clients. Always maintain confidentiality.

- Practice active listening and empathy. Make eye contact, demonstrate that you are listening, and never criticize or react negatively to clients expressing their feelings. These actions show that you are fully present with your client at that moment. Being fully present is an ongoing goal for practitioners, a goal that is more easily met when you consistently do your own work.

- Be patient with your client, yourself, and the process of EFT. Remember the earlier statement, "Sometimes the fastest way to get there is to slow down."

Everything you say and do and how you react to everything your client says and does affects your rapport with your client. With some clients, rapport is simple to establish. Remember, though, that rapport is an *ongoing* important part of the practitioner-client relationship. It can also be lost. Assessing the level of the relationship between the two of you is a constant part of working with clients.

Practitioner Self-Care

Although most of this resource book is intended to offer you a comprehensive understanding of advanced skills and techniques to aid in the practice of EFT with others, for the practitioner self-care is essential to ethical practice. Practitioner self-care is emphasized in most training and certification programs. Dr. Fred Gallo writes, "The health of the therapist is important for the health of the client. Energy resonates. When the therapist is in a state of health, the health resonates and positively affects the client" (2013).

Those who have dedicated their lives to helping others in a therapeutic capacity often have the tendency to give of their resources, skills, and talents in a way that can become detrimental to their own emotional and physical health. Though usually well intentioned, this is never sustainable. Developing a consistent program of self-care is vital to your continued efficacy as a practitioner.

There are many aspects to practicing good self-care. Continued use of the Personal Peace Procedure, altered and expanded as you go, is one effective way to systematically address your memories, events, and emotions. Our personal work is never finished; self-care is an ongoing and evolving process. Doing your own emotional work will have positive effects for your health, as well as provide a sense of peace and a lack of internal conflict that will serve the health of your clients and your practice. Daily tapping can resolve your daily annoyances, reduce your frustrations, provide strength to deal with challenges, alleviate stress, help you decompress after working with clients, and continue to add to your personal health and resilience. During sessions with others, be mindful and observant of your emotions, thoughts, and potential triggers to address during your daily tapping.

Good self-care is multifaceted. The following are practices that the authors find important:

- First, continue to do your own emotional work. Consistently address issues, triggers, negative thoughts, and negative emotions. The less of these negatives you have the more it is possible to be really present with your client, get "out of your own way," and allow intuition to grow.

- Consider swapping sessions with colleagues. This not only helps you personally, but also gives you the opportunity to see how other professionals work.

- Do what you need to do to protect your own physical health.

- Get enough sleep! How many times have we heard that one? It remains important. According to Dr. Merrill Mitler, a sleep expert and neuroscientist at the National Institutes of Health (NIH), "Loss of sleep impairs your higher levels of reasoning, problem-solving, and attention to detail. It affects growth and stress hormones, our immune system, appetite, breathing, blood pressure, and cardiovascular health" (National Institutes of Health, 2013).

- Engage in hobbies and other activities that do not involve your practice, your clients, or your work. Participating in a hobby that you love helps build confidence, enhance creativity, and increase job performance, and raises the levels of neurotransmitters in your brain. Dr. Gabriela Cora, a psychiatrist and managing partner of the Florida Neuroscience Center, writes, "Making time for enjoyable activities stimulates parts of the brain associated with creative and positive thinking. You become emotionally and intellectually more motivated" (Zimmerman, 2007).

- Move around. Our bodies are meant to move. You've probably heard the statement that "sitting is the new smoking" in regard to our health. Walk or stretch between clients. Move when you are on the computer. With laptops and Wi-Fi, it is easier to change rooms or chairs or use a stand-up desk. Ann's favorite technique when needing to be on the computer for lengthy periods is to set a timer for 50 minutes. She uses those 50 minutes for focused project time. When the bell goes off, she gets up for 10 minutes to do something totally unrelated: play with the dog, stretch, do a brief chore (or part of one), or take a short walk. It is amazing how much more focused you can be when you use this simple timer technique. Karin's method is to stand up and simply do a few squats every hour.

- Continue to develop and add to your skills. EFT is an evolving modality. There is always more to learn. Continue to seek out and participate in educational opportunities so you refine your skills, which will make you a better practitioner and add to your professional network and available resources.

- Practice setting healthy boundaries. Boundaries are essential to the ethical practice of anyone in a helping field. Setting boundaries means preserving your personal and recuperative time, sticking to the appointments you set with your clients, maintaining a personal life that is separate from your practice, managing relationships with your clients that are therapeutically appropriate, and practicing healthy spatial boundaries when in your practice (e.g., how close to sit to your client, and asking permission before tapping on a client).

- Notice when you are being negatively affected at the moment it happens. For example, one foster mother, whom we'll call Louise, has learned to use EFT "to stay calm, not want to retaliate, and stay out of the psychological games kids can play." Louise sometimes uses EFT when she can hear things between her foster kids begin to escalate in another room. That is, she gets herself ready to be an effective foster parent before checking on what is happening. Her foster kids are lucky to have such a dedicated and determined caregiver. Even if you don't have your own or foster kids to help you identify your triggers, most people have someone who pushes their "buttons." These buttons can be disconnected through EFT so we are no longer vulnerable to people finding them. People can't push something that no longer exists.

Self-care is essential for maximizing your ability to do your best work. EFT practitioners and those in other helping professions often identify so much with the role of helping others that, although they know self-care is important, it is frequently last on the priority list. Schedule you into your day by putting self-care activities on your schedule.

The Successful EFT Practice

In addition to all of the skills you've developed and that you continue to develop, as an effective EFT practitioner, you must build and maintain your business. If you don't let people know where you are and what you do, you will stop yourself from some opportunities to share your skills. Many times, practitioners want to focus on the tapping end of the EFT practice and forget to put time and energy into the nuts and bolts of having a business.

Traits of a Good Practitioner

One of the most common obstacles to creating an EFT practice is the desire for perfection before beginning. Keep in mind that "done" is better than perfect. You can improve as you go. Stating Emile Coué's mantra, "Every day in every way I am getting better and better" is a terrific exercise to begin every day. Starting a new business venture can seem overwhelming. Take it "one step at a time." Pick an area you want to improve or a business task that seems manageable and comfortable for you.

Tapping is a wonderful tool; do not forget that it is important to tap for your own fears and blocks. If we each waited until we were perfect at something before attempting it, we would never move forward—on anything. Moving forward does not mean we forge ahead casually and blindly even if we are ill prepared. It means we allow ourselves to learn while we are helping others. In the book *EFT and Beyond* (Bruner and Bullough, 2009, p. 65), Ann writes:

> A professional has confidence in his or her abilities because she has done the work it takes to achieve excellence. A professional is comfortable in her own skin; and has clarity on who she really is...don't go where you don't belong. Get lots of practice. Swap sessions with other EFT users. Train with someone who has lots of experience with EFT and has developed a

successful practice. Getting consultation and mentoring from someone like that is invaluable. With experience and good rapport, in-depth listening, and a terrific sense of timing you can help guide the client to even deeper levels.

It is important to study EFT in depth with good teachers as well as on your own. It is important that we all are careful and respectful while we use EFT to help others and ourselves. It's important to schedule sessions with other practitioners to deal with our own complex issues and blocks to success. It is important to have a depth of knowledge and a goal of continual learning. It is *not* important to wait until we are perfect. Obviously, we never get to perfection; no one is perfect.

The best EFT Practitioners continue to say things like:

- Correct me if I don't have these words quite right.

- How do you describe that in your own words?

- If I get off track here, please tell me.

- Change my words to make the phrase (statement, questions, etc.) sound true for you.

- I'm not sure this specific EFT technique will work, but let's give it a try.

- I'm not here to give you advice; I'm here to help you help yourself with EFT.

- Are we on the right track here or is there a better direction?

- We have two (or several) directions we can go. What seems the most important to you to start?

- I've gotten lost in this "tangle." Let's stop a minute and straighten it out. Are you saying…?

- If I didn't understand what the word X (fear, panicked, angry, etc.) meant, how would you describe it to me?

- Okay, you said "this," now you've said "that." I'm confused; can you clear that up for me?

- Did this session meet your expectations or is there another direction you feel would be better?

These types of questions or statements elicit feedback that can be invaluable to help guide sessions. You will get what you need by asking clients, not by knowing how to address every client and his or her issues perfectly. When you get into a situation in which you don't know what to do, be assured that all EFT practitioners have been in that same position. Go back to basics and use traditional EFT concepts, such as asking questions to get more specific data or ideas. Even the best EFT practitioners have suddenly found themselves thinking, "Now what?"

Address your insecurities honestly and directly. Address your skills and strengths just as honestly and directly in your EFT self-practice. For example, see what comes up as you tap on:

- *Even though I'm worried that I don't know enough, I have trained and read and watched and studied for hours. I can share what I do know to help others in my own way.*

- *Even though I'm scared I won't do it correctly, I have prepared and practiced for many hours. I have tapped on many, many of my own issues; I can focus on clients and follow their lead. I am doing the best I can in service of others.*

- *Even though I am no expert, yet, I'm sharing this tool to help others and I am grateful that I can learn while I'm helping others.*

Create variations on these statements that feel true for you. Pay attention to your body sensations as you say the words. Asking yourself when was another time that you felt that way can lead to events that are foundational to your fears. It is a truism that you will never be perfect; you will never know everything. Fortunately, no one else expects you to. What they do expect is for you to be a warm, caring, present, honest—real—human being.

Ann, Karin, and Kari have each been in sessions with clients in which they have been totally stumped. Even after hundreds of clients, there will be times when all that comes to mind is "I don't have a clue where to go from here" or "What do I do now?" Something practitioners often forget is that clients can feel incredibly uncomfortable facing what they perceive to be their weaknesses, flaws, embarrassments, and limitations in front of someone else. Clients who believe they are baring their souls before someone who never has doubts, never struggles, always knows the right thing to say, and for whom things always work out well are clients who are likely to feel isolated from their practitioners during sessions.

On the other hand, when practitioners admit, even embrace, their limitations, clients are invited to appreciate the reality that we are all in the same boat in life. We all have doubts. We all struggle at times. We all search for the right thing to say and yet later we might believe that we said the totally wrong thing. We all experience situations that do not work out the way we want them to. Given that we are all basically on the same path, trying to find our way through situations, relationships, and experiences that we find challenging, we practitioners have an opportunity to be amused and informed by our own limitations and mistakes, as well as to be compassionate with clients about their fears and frustrations.

After getting information from the client, Karin may say, "Give me a moment to determine which EFT technique would be the best in this circumstance." This gives Karin a moment to assess as well as ask any additional questions before moving on. Clients have reported that this makes them feel heard, that they are not getting "one-size-fits-all" EFT, are more comfortable with Karin's expertise, and feel safer in trying something new.

One of the benefits of getting stuck in sessions or of making mistakes is that we then get to be role models for clients regarding how to deal with sticky situations. The point of being practitioners is not to demonstrate how wonderful we are to impress our clients (or anyone else), but to invite clients to become more aware of their own worth as people, even in the midst of their difficulties, fears, anxieties, embarrassments, and struggles. They don't have to prove their worth to us. In order to accept them wherever they are, we need to first accept ourselves where we are.

The Five Most Important Marketing Strategies

Marketing your EFT practice is one of the components of success. Everyone finds marketing challenging, even those who are good at it. We will give you some options to begin the process. Begin by choosing the three things you are most comfortable doing, and then the next three, the next three, and so on. Start with the ones that you might enjoy doing or the ones that don't seem so difficult. Just start. Even if you decide to outsource the tasks, just start. Somewhere.

The most important marketing strategies are:

1. Get business cards.

2. Create a website, even if it's a single "brochure" page about your services and benefits.

3. Create an "elevator speech."

4. Talk to people—lots of people, everywhere, all the time.

5. Start! Anywhere. Done is better than perfect.

1. Get Business Cards

Business cards are an often overlooked, yet incredibly powerful marketing tool. You can carry them with you, hand them to people you meet or who show interest in you or your practice, and use them to network with potential clients and other professionals. Business cards allow you to leave something with the people you meet that features you and your practice. By giving them your card, you won't have to rely on their memory or motivation to find your listing should they decide to contact you.

Your business name can feature your own name or you can choose a name that you believe represents how you approach EFT. Examples would be: Tap Your Potential, Be What You Want, Supportive EFT, Embracing Life, and Creative Options. Do a search on the Internet first to see if someone else is using the name you choose. Although many people do not trademark their business names, it is still good practice to make sure no one else is currently using your desired name.

There are many websites that allow you to design and order business cards online. You can also hire a company at a reasonable cost (one very reasonable site is Fiverr.com) to help you develop a "look." You can put your picture with your contact information on your card so people can more easily remember you. More important than the visual design of your business card, however, is to make sure

135

your name, phone number, and e-mail addresses are accurate and included on the card. Keep it simple; don't try to put too much on your card.

Handing out your cards is no guarantee that anyone will call you. The key reason for sharing your card with people is to get their card or contact information. Follow up with a phone call or e-mail about what you talked about and your willingness to help. There is a marketing truism that says, "There is a fortune in the follow up." Pick up the phone. Follow up with that interested networking contact. Ask how you can help them. When your new contact is a potential referral source, be sure to stay in touch; send them information you discover that you think they would find interesting; when appropriate, send a referral to them. Two-way referral sources are valuable practice builders.

2. Create a Website

In a world of fast-growing technology, websites are the standard in marketing your practice or business. There are many helpful hints for building an effective website. The following will mention a few tips that we have found particularly important in the helping professions.

Look at other sites. A good place to start developing your website is to look at other sites and write down what you don't like as well as what you do like. This will help you and your designer(s) choose the best design for you. Be specific if you have a strong feeling one way or another. This will make the actual development of your site with the choices of colors, fonts, and styles easier. Check with people familiar with how websites work, though, regarding the importance of some of the details that have attracted your attention.

One web design client of Karin's became so concerned about the way a single letter looked in the font of her choice that she wanted to create an entirely new font. This would have wasted time and money when it wasn't important for the efficacy of her site. Throughout the process of developing your website, you can choose and demand whatever you want, but remember that the purpose of a good website is to help your new clients know more about you and be comfortable with you. Keep it simple as you begin. You can always alter and add to your website later as you learn more about what your clients would like and need.

Know what your audience needs to know. Clearly identify, quickly, on your home page, what your website is about. Keep the home page simple. Keep it focused on your reader. What pain or problem do you help them solve?

Write your web copy and choose which website buttons (links to other pages) to include based on what your clients want to know, not what you think they should know. How do you figure out what clients want to know? When writing your copy, answer questions that clients often ask you before they agree to see you and/or during the first session.

- What questions do you remember that you wanted answers for before you first tried EFT?
- What questions do clients and others often ask you?

- How would you like clients to contact you and/or make appointments?
- What happens in an EFT session with you?
- What are your rates and how will your clients pay you?

Although you want to have information about yourself to create credibility, the *focus of the website should be on the benefits clients gain* from working with you.

Make color and graphic choices based on how you would like to be perceived. If you are very spiritual, you can use photographs and graphics that are more ethereal. If you want to be considered in a more restrained and professional market, make your site more standard. You won't have the opportunity to explain what you meant to convey on your website to each person who visits it, so be aware of the perceptions you are inviting people who visit your website to experience. Get feedback from your current clients; they will have personal likes and dislikes. Ask them if they went to the website and if anything on it was a factor in leading them to contact you. Ask if there was other information they wished had been on your site. Corporations pay for focus groups to help them understand what works on their websites and what doesn't; your clients can be your focus group.

Keep your website simple and uncluttered. Make it clear what the site is all about. The cliché "Don't make me think" applies to websites. That is, potential clients often want to get a quick impression of benefits you are conveying—with the emphasis on quick. Make sure a viewer can tell within seconds what your business offers them.

One professionally created website had little impact on potential clients. When an experienced practitioner reviewed the website, she commented, "You appear to be offering knowledge to your potential clients. In contrast, I often find that websites offering compassion for people who are distressed are more effective."

Potential clients want to feel better; they probably already have more information than they know what to do with because they do not know how to integrate it into their lives. Your website should show your understanding and compassion for their problems. We all benefit from being treated compassionately and learning to treat ourselves compassionately.

Get a professional photograph. Provide clients with a quality and professional photo of yourself on your website. Before stepping into this unfamiliar world of using energy techniques on their issues, some potential clients want as much information as they can get, including what you look like. Clients are choosing you, your talent, and your ability to understand and have solutions for their problems.

Don't like your picture? Congratulations, you have identified an issue for you to tap on. Clients are more likely to engage your services if they see the person whom they're hiring. Make sure your picture conveys the real you with your compassion. Ask someone else who understands you and what makes you unique to help you choose the photo that best conveys your positive qualities, especially if you are one of the many of us who have a difficult time imagining putting a picture of ourselves on our site.

Karin suggests making your picture as natural as possible and not staged. Don't use strange head angles or fake backgrounds. Potential clients want to see the person they'll see when they walk in the door (or work with on the phone/Skype). Keep your photo current. Someone out there is looking for you to help them. Be professional and be real.

Suggested basic buttons for your website:

- Home/Welcome Page with your picture and the benefits of working with you and a compassionate statement that shows your understanding of their problem.

- What is EFT?

- About Me (or Us or etc.)

- What to Expect

- Client Testimonials

- Contact Me (and put this information or a link to it on every page).

Product pricing. Whether to put your fees on the site is an individual decision. Some marketers say it should be there and other marketers say the price discussion should be made at an initial contact. This could also be dependent on the type of services you offer.

Include a disclaimer. A disclaimer should be very clear on your website. Everyone's disclaimer is going to be individual to him or her. You could consult an attorney knowledgeable about being a practitioner and EFT. Put your statement at the bottom of your home page, contact page, or on its own page with a separate button. Disclaimers are a necessary part of informed consent and are highly recommended. In your disclaimer, you will want to mention that, rather than making promises about the outcome of treatment, you are inviting clients to learn ways to resolve their problems. That is, you are focused on the process of treatment rather than guaranteeing a specific end result. You might want to mention that, through EFT, clients often discover solutions to their issues that are very different from the solutions they envisioned before beginning treatment.

Search Engine Optimization (SEO). SEO refers to the process of making a website compatible with the results ranking system used by Internet search engines, such as Google, Yahoo, or Bing. When you type a search term into a Google search bar, for example, the results that display on your screen are not random. The search engine selects those sites based on which of all the sites on the World Wide Web match the search criteria the best. This is determined by the SEO process, most of which happens in the programming and technical end of your site. Building a website does not mean people can type in a search term and your site will be in the top listings. SEO is a complicated service that is not automatic. The first step is to register your website URL with Google, Yahoo, and as many of the other search engines as you want (you can start at www.google.com/webmasters). Although there are many service providers that offer assistance in this area, SEO is rarely included with website design and development, unless specifically requested.

Don't copy without permission. Images on websites and those that come up in search engine image searches (such as Google Images) are copyrighted. Do not use them without permission. This includes clipart. There are many EFT sites that will allow you to utilize their photos and images if you include a link back to their website. Examples of the kind of statement to include are: "Image with permission from www.HowToTap.com" or "Text from www.FromtheDeskofAnnAdams.com." The helping profession is a highly integrity-based profession. Be aware that even if your use of someone else's words or images was unintentional, it can still appear to be "stealing." The EFT community is very generous; ask permission, and if you get permission, give credit. There are several websites that offer thousands of inexpensive or free images. Find something unique and meaningful that represents your business.

3. Create an Elevator Speech

Ann Adams stresses the importance of an effective elevator speech in her *Insider's Guide to Marketing Your EFT Practice* as an effective way to "pitch" EFT and your practice. The term "elevator speech" refers to a 20–30 second marketing script you can use when you have an opportunity to answer questions quickly about what you do. It is called an "elevator speech" because when riding in an elevator, you normally have less than 30 seconds to answer when someone asks you a question. Developing a short marketing script, and having it memorized, can make talking about yourself, EFT, and your practice much less stressful. The less stress you experience in that moment, the more effectively you can communicate!

When developing your own elevator speech, remember to keep your words generic, concise, and informative without going into detail. The idea of an elevator speech is to communicate value and pique interest. It can also serve as a way to introduce yourself.

These 30 seconds of information are usually most effective when they contain:

1. A brief one-sentence description of what you do.

2. A success story.

3. Where the person can find more information.

Example: *I'm here for an EFT conference. EFT is a stress relief technique that combines a kind of talk therapy with acupressure. EFT reduces the stress and other negative emotions around unpleasant events from your past. I was recently at a party and a woman was deeply upset about her husband getting a job in another state. She made an appointment with me to try EFT. After one session, she reported that her entire outlook about the situation had changed and she now looked forward to the move.*

Example: *I work with people to help them get over their blocks to success. I use a technique called EFT, which is like talk therapy while you are lightly touching acu-*

pressure points on your face and upper body. I know it sounds a bit out there, but it really works. I just worked with a teenager who failed her driving test nine times and after one session, she passed it. If you want to know more, here's my card. It's nice to meet you.

Example: *I've been involved in helping others overcome traumatic events and self-defeating beliefs for 35+ years. One of the most effective techniques I've studied is EFT or Emotional Freedom Techniques. I was the administrator of a children's residential treatment program and I found that this method worked so well that I've spent the last 15 years training people how to use EFT easily with their clients. Not only does EFT work well with all existing therapeutic techniques; it's great as self-help too. Here's my card with a link to learn how you can use it for yourself. I'd love to hear your feedback. Let me know how I can help you.*

It is best to memorize three or four different types of presentation to have options that can relate to your current surroundings and the interests of the person you are talking to. It's also a good idea to have a few longer "speeches" that might be useful for various opportunities. The idea is, as the Boy Scout's motto emphasizes, "Be prepared." The best way to be prepared is to practice, practice, practice.

Anne Baber and Lynne Waymon, authors of *Make Your Contacts Count: Networking Know-How for Business and Career Success,* explain that people usually think networking is about talking and taking, when, in truth, networking is about teaching and giving.

Teach people:

- Who you are.
- What to come to you for.
- What you're good at.
- What kinds of opportunities to send your way.
- What they can count on you for.

Give people what they are looking for by:

- Listening to others in a way that is generous so that you can help them find what they need.
- Offering resources that might include other contacts you know.

Pat Drew, human resources director at the *New York Times* for 20 years and manager of training at the New York Psychiatric Institute of Columbia University, believes that effective elevator speeches answer the following questions (Drew, 2012):

- What do you do? What is your passion?
- What is the need or pain your services address?
- What are the benefits?
- What is your credibility?
- What is your goal?

An effective elevator speech is not only a valuable marketing tool for your practice, but can also play an important role in building bridges to those who are skeptical of or have no knowledge of EFT. A well-rehearsed elevator speech that communicates value and arouses interest in the listener can expand the venues in which you can introduce others to EFT, providing you an excellent tool to move individuals closer to that "maybe I'll try it" moment. Speaking confidently and briefly can increase your credibility, making it more likely that the person will agree to give this EFT "stuff" a chance.

An effective elevator speech would be expected to spark interest and invite the listener to ask questions. It is not the time to explain as much about EFT as you know. Each person will have a different angle of interest and by waiting for their questions after you finish your short introduction, people will let you know their particular curiosity. If you are talking about EFT in a way that is well thought out, you are likely to feel more confident in introducing EFT to others, especially when there isn't much time. Your knowledge and confidence will contribute to your credibility and will communicate volumes more than the actual words you speak.

After giving your elevator speech, offer your business card. The other person can take your card or not, just as potential clients can choose to come see you or not. You can feel confident that you represented yourself and your practice in a way that was professional, understandable, and effective. As noted previously, the major goal of giving your business card to other people is to get their business card. Effective business people follow up every contact by phone or e-mail with a brief message. *Successful businesses are created through follow-up.* We repeat this because it is so important: Successful businesses are created through follow-up. Don't expect someone to call you from the card; you follow up with them whether by e-mail, snail mail, or phone conversation.

4. Talk to People

Talk to people, everywhere, all the time. Pick up the phone or go see people. Personal contact in which you share what you do and you actually ask for business is the number-one way to build a business.

5. Start!

Start now! Done is better than perfect. As you continue to practice, learn, and expand, you will find that truly every day in every way you are indeed getting better!

There are many ways to market your business, and information is widely available via the Internet, books, DVDs, workshops, and more. Start marketing within your comfort zone; choose methods that are easiest for you, and just start. Although in today's world having a website is expected, simply putting up a website and waiting for the phone to ring is not effective. One challenge is there is *so much* out there with the Internet gurus now it is easy to chase after each new "bright shiny object." If you are new to establishing your business, find a couple of basic marketing books in your field and implement the information in them before you branch out with more options. Use what you already have first. Basic marketing techniques still apply.

Perhaps the most powerful way initially, which is a way that evokes terror in many hearts, is to pick up the phone and call people—the people you have met and networked with, other professionals that could be a part of your referral network, and other connections that could benefit your practice or business. That phone really doesn't weigh 50 pounds—really. Tell people what you are doing (remember those various elevator speeches), ask them what are their biggest challenges, ask if there are any ways in which you can help them. Sometimes people appreciate the chance to ask questions of someone in the helping field; give them that opportunity.

For example, people might ask, "What do I do if I have a brother (sister, mother, father, friend, partner) who is drinking and I don't know how to help him (her)?" You could answer that by saying, "I can hear that you're worried about your brother (whomever) and I would be happy to help you deal with what you're experiencing in this situation. Maybe if you feel less stressed by this person's problems, you will be more clear about what you want to do if this person keeps drinking." Another person might ask, "Why am I so afraid of talking in front of groups? I totally lose my focus, can't think of anything, and look like an idiot." You might answer by saying, "Actually, different people have different reasons for feeling anxious. I'd be happy to help you get to the bottom of your anxiety." If you can't help, however, and you know someone else who could help with their issue, refer them.

Don't forget to ask them if they know anyone whom they believe needs your help. Network, everywhere. Creating a network of mutual referral sources is a helpful way to increase your business.

In addition to the five most important marketing strategies we emphasized here, there are two other steps that can help build your EFT practice:

1. Start some kind of social media involvement and update it regularly.

2. Submit articles and stories to EFT websites that allow articles by others to be posted. This strategy can be powerful as it makes you visible to a broader audience than you can reach on your own.

Choosing how to market your practice is an evolving process. It will grow and change as you do. You can always improve it as long as you have begun—somewhere. There are some resources available at PractitionerResources.EFTuniverse.com that can help you. Ann has a basic marketing book as well, *Insiders' Guide to Marketing Your EFT Practice* (see MarketingYourEFTPractice.com).

Volunteer for Group Presentations

A very engaging and possibly profitable marketing practice involves conducting free group introductions. It is a wonderful way to get EFT out into the world and at the same time demonstrate your talents. We suggest you initially only volunteer to provide free introductory workshops to groups with which you have a local or personal connection. Some examples are:

- Women's groups.
- Men's groups.
- Senior communities.
- Self-help groups.
- Law of Attraction groups.
- Professional groups of which you are a member.
- Adult continuing education courses.

Practice your presentation beforehand. As a friend once said, "Tapping can allay your public speaking fears, but it can't make you good." Solid preparation will improve your presentation and also help you feel confident. Record your talk and listen to it, noting places you would change. Practice on a friend who will be an appreciative audience. While you're making your presentation to your friend, have something nearby to write on so you can make notes. Your friend can ask you questions, which could help you elaborate on your ideas or cut out parts that are less effective.

It is best to memorize the opening 5 minutes of your presentation. Memorizing your opening gives you time to get acclimated to your audience and overcome any public speaking uneasiness. (Remember to tap beforehand for any fears you have about public speaking.) You probably don't want to memorize the rest of your presentation because you are likely to sound more spontaneous and engaging if you are talking informally about something you know rather than reciting a speech.

Keep your presentations simple. Don't try to teach an entire EFT class in 20 minutes, or even 90 minutes. Narrow down what you're trying to convey to your audience to what is manageable in the time frame allotted to you. Most speakers make the mistake of giving too much information for the listener to take in. Have three to seven key points. Then, as the old adage goes, tell them what you are going to tell them, tell them, then tell them what you told them.

Generally, you don't have to speak the entire time. Leave time for questions. Some people in audiences will not ask questions out loud (because they might have a fear of speaking in public), so give an option to ask a question in writing. Take index cards and pass them out to everyone in the audience. Pass out pencils to people who don't have anything to write with so they have an opportunity to write their questions. Ask people to write their questions before you begin the presentation or while you're talking. Collect the cards at the end of your presentation, read the questions or comments, and respond. Most people are far more interested in presentations where the presenter is interested in their questions and opinions.

Be aware that if you open yourself up to questions and comments, some people might challenge you and say this sounds crazy, useless, or unreasonable. Often you can connect with these people by telling them about any time in the past when you wondered about whether or not some portion of EFT would work, or maybe you were sure that EFT wouldn't work at all. You could say something similar to: "I used to have some of the same questions, but I changed my mind after I learned how powerful a treatment EFT can be by experiencing it. I invite everyone to be open to learning about it, but I know that some people take a while to consider trying something that is so unfamiliar to them. Take all the time you need to learn about it. If I can help in any way, I'd be happy to do that."

Forms, Policies, and Procedures

Although forms and procedures are rarely the first thing new practitioners think about, creating your forms and procedures is one of the first things for you to develop. As you begin your EFT practice, you will need to make sure you cross your *t*'s and dot your *i*'s, especially as you grow your client base beyond friends and family. Your procedures will help you maintain professionalism and boundaries in events that are unusual or challenging in your practice. They will ensure that your clients understand that you are operating professionally and ethically.

Create your forms and establish your procedures before you have your first paying client. Don't wait until your first client is sitting in your office to start thinking about your practice's policies and procedures! However, not all policies and procedures need to be made public on your website. A key purpose of developing your own policies and procedures is addressing your own choices regarding how you do business. Keep in mind that your policies and procedures don't need to be perfect either; they are often a work in progress.

Answering questions for yourself before you start your business will help you have an answer formulated for almost any question or eventuality that comes up. It will make it easy then to respond to a challenging situation with "My business policy is…" Recognize, of course, that no practitioners ever think of all the questions clients might ask them. Be prepared to occasionally answer, "I never thought about that before. What a good question. I'll consider it and ask my mentors (fellow practitioners, someone) to learn more about that issue." The following list addresses information you might want to include in your policies and procedures:

- **Appointments**
  - How does a client make an appointment? Online? Call?
  - How long are your appointments?
  - What do clients do if they need to cancel or reschedule an appointment? Is there a relevant time frame for canceling or rescheduling? (e.g., 24, 48, or 72 hours before an appointment)
  - What do you do if someone misses an appointment? Are they charged the whole fee or part of the fee? Do they get one free "pass" per year for which they are not charged, but they are charged for subsequent missed sessions? How do you reschedule?

o   How will clients be notified of cancellations, rescheduling, office clo-sures due to inclement weather, in case you, the practitioner, becomes ill, or in case you have to deal with a personal emergency? How will you make up these times?

- **Fees**

  o   How much do your sessions cost? Do you offer any discounts for book-ing larger numbers of sessions at once?

  o   How will you accept payment? Cash, personal checks, debit or credit cards, PayPal, link to pay online, or in person, etc.?

  o   Do you accept bartering/trades?

  o   Do you wish to offer a sliding scale or any assistance to those with financial difficulties? If you offer sliding-scale places to some clients, is there a limit regarding how many clients you will accept at one time who need a sliding scale? Some practitioners will accept five (or may-be 10) sliding-scale clients at one time and, if someone else calls for sliding-scale sessions while all those positions are being filled by other clients who need a sliding scale, you can tell potential new clients ei-ther a) to wait until a sliding-scale opportunity opens because previ-ous clients attained their goals and completed their treatment, or b) to schedule sessions less often than they would desire because they could pay for some sessions but not frequent sessions. Alternatively, some clients choose to come for shorter sessions. For example, some clients might be able to pay half your fee and you could offer to see them for half the length of your typical sessions.

  o   How are clients billed and when do they pay?

- **Client-Practitioner Relationship**

  o   Do you accept gifts and social invitations from clients? (There are rules in some professional organizations regarding this.)

  o   How do you handle seeing a client at a social gathering or in public?

  o   How do you handle clients and social media interaction? (It is com-mon for private practice professionals to employ a social media policy. You might find it beneficial to develop a social media policy to avoid complications due to being vague in this area.)

  o   What, if any, contact is permitted from clients between sessions? Can they e-mail you, call your office, etc.?

  o   How will you handle dual relationships? ("Dual relationships" refer to practitioner-client relationships in which two individuals are also connected in another way. For example, if Donna is a practitioner and offers to see Mariah, her housekeeper, for sessions, this is a dual relationship. Dual relationships are ethically grey areas, especially in

145

situations in which a practitioner is not also a licensed therapist. We aren't saying not to use EFT on your mom, sister, friend, lady from church, or even housekeeper; we are cautioning that not everyone can maintain the high levels of boundaries necessary to effectively manage these types of dual relationships on an ongoing basis. Practitioners do themselves a favor by considering the potential ramifications of having more than one type of relationship with a person for whom you are providing treatment. This presents an opportunity to take advantage of your referral network!)

- **Records**
    - o How will you keep client records? (This includes any notes, forms, and other information.)
    - o Who has access to these records? How are they protected?
    - o How long will you keep records after a client stops using your services? Is there licensing or state law about this?
    - o How will you dispose of these records in a way that protects your clients' privacy and maintains professional confidentiality?

Once you have clarified your practice's policies and procedures, and answered these and other questions about how you will run your practice and how you will professionally interact with clients, you get to decide how you will communicate this information to your clients. Some practitioners choose to offer information online, or as part of the "Frequently Asked Questions" or "Before Your Session" sections of their website. Others choose to include this information in their intake documents to ensure that every client has a chance to read the policies and procedures. No matter how you decide to make your policies and procedures accessible to your clients, do develop them. They are vital to the continued professionalism of your practice; they can prevent misunderstandings or misplaced expectations.

Intake Forms

Intake forms are a valuable and prudent way to begin a client-practitioner relationship. Intake forms provide you with a mechanism to ensure that clients have the opportunity to read pertinent policies and procedures for your practice, as well as any disclaimers. Forms are an effective way for you, the practitioner, to gather information about your client. Your intake forms will allow you to gather basic information including the client's name, contact information, emergency contact information, clients' goals in coming to you, previous treatment, medications being taken, and so on.

It might also be helpful to include questions about the client's religious or spiritual beliefs, or any other specifics you may wish to know before beginning sessions. In the case of understanding a client's religious beliefs, some practitioners find this helpful because it allows them to tailor the language of their sessions to be compatible with that particular client's beliefs, and, it is to be hoped, avoid awkward or offensive assumptions.

You can tailor your intake forms to assess the information you find most helpful in your practice. You might state at the top that clients have the option of not telling you some of the information you are requesting. Whatever they do not fill out provides you with information about these clients. Among other things, they are revealing that they have trust issues and/or vulnerability issues regarding the topics they omit. Whatever clients do or refuse to do provides you with useful information. Clients come to you because they want to get some things figured out. They don't come unless they need help somewhere. Be aware, however, that a client might refuse initially to tell you about the particular area in which they need help; this is not usual, but it does happen.

The Energy Healer's Toolkit created by Donna Eden and David Feinstein, which is available at PractitionerResources.EFTuniverse.com, contains all the forms you will need to start a practice.

Informed Consent and Disclaimers

Although your intake form questions can be written in a way that gathers the information you find pertinent to your work with clients, be sure that you have explained to your clients what your scope of practice is, what EFT is intended to do, and what EFT is not intended to do. If you are not in a medical profession and are not licensed to treat individuals in a clinical practice, and thus will work with EFT in the scope of an EFT practice only, be sure to explain your legal status in your state. Adhere to the scope of practice that is appropriate.

Your clients need to know your level of licensure and/or certification. Be aware of the language you use to describe your practice and the services you offer. For example, if you are not licensed in a medical profession or to work with clients on a clinical level, in most states you cannot refer to your practice as "therapy" or "psychology." This means that, although referring to yourself as a therapist or as someone who offers "energy psychology" to your clients might sound nice to you, there are legal issues involved. Research your state and any local legal requirements for your type of practice.

Your intake and other forms, as well as your website, need to provide a clear explanation that EFT is not intended to replace care or treatment from qualified health providers. Unless you are legally qualified to do so, state that you are not qualified to: diagnose or treat illness; make recommendations concerning pharmaceutical drugs, medication, or surgery; or handle medical emergencies.

Likewise, if you are working with minors in your practice, be sure to have a parent or guardian sign appropriate consent forms. Check with your state and professional guidelines about the information necessary to work with minors. Among other things, make sure that the parent who seeks your help has permission to take the child to any type of health provider. That is, situations involving legally separated or divorced parents may need to be handled differently, as there may be a court decree that only one parent can give consent for a child to receive treatment. When a divorced parent brings a child to you for treatment, have the parent sign a form that documents that he or she has the right to seek your services for the child.

As a practitioner, it is your responsibility to research the laws and requirements of your particular state and make sure that you are following all the appropriate laws and guidelines. The laws can be complex; make sure you are aware of what impacts your practice. It is helpful to talk with other practitioners to learn what challenges they are dealing with so you don't have to reinvent the wheel in your own practice.

Ethics

In any of the helping professions, and in any form of a private practice, there are ethical concerns to be considered. When working with others in any capacity, our first priority should be to do no harm. It is beyond the scope of this book to cover all of the ethical considerations for each type of practice; there are a variety of ethics codes available for all licensed professions. Be sure to review the appropriate code of ethics for your profession as it applies to alternative techniques. We also encourage you to become familiar with the code of ethics from the appropriate organization for your license, credentials, and/or training.

If you are unlicensed and practicing EFT as a practitioner only, there are codes of ethics written by various organizations supporting energy-based therapies that you can reference. These include AAMET (Association for the Advancement of Meridian Energy Techniques), ACEP (Association for Comprehensive Energy Psychology), EFT Universe, and ACHP (Alternative and Complementary Healthcare Professionals). These organizations also include ethics training to help you understand the basics of practicing responsibly as a practitioner.

There are books on ethics that can also provide you with guidance. The authors of this coursebook particularly recommend *Ethics Handbook for Energy Healing Practitioners,* by David Feinstein with Donna Eden, and *Creating Healing Relationships: Professional Standards for Energy Therapy Practitioners,* by Dorothea Hover-Kramer.

The following are important ethical issues to consider.

Confidentiality

It is your ethical responsibility to protect the confidentiality of your clients, regardless of the scope of your practice. Ensuring that your clients' information is protected applies to both written and electronic records. This involves how you will dispose of client records in a way that protects each client's private information. It also means that you will refrain from discussing, writing about, or recording any sessions without the written consent of your client.

Referrals

Ensure that your clients have had the appropriate medical workups or refer them to the appropriate medical professionals if the symptoms for which they are seeking relief are medical/physical, or if there is any doubt that they are beyond the scope of your knowledge, or if the condition could in any way be life threatening. Work only with clients with whom you are qualified to do so.

Maintain Professional Relationships

Be wary of dual relationships, and ensure that you are practicing appropriate boundaries in your client-practitioner relationships. Practitioners have the responsibility to protect clients from issues related to participating in treatment. Be aware that clients sometimes misinterpret practitioners' intentions and imagine that practitioners might want to be friends when practitioners are being professionally considerate rather than being personally friendly. It will be helpful for clients if you clarify that you are asking about clients' issues to make it possible to provide better treatment for them, not simply to learn about them. In the process of providing treatment for clients, you have opportunities to gather information that could be used to exploit clients. Not only do you need to keep that information locked up between sessions, but you also need to monitor yourself to make sure you never use your professional relationships to exploit clients emotionally, financially, or sexually.

Learn Applicable Licensing and Governmental Guidelines and Regulations

There are significant numbers of EFT practitioners who do not use EFT under a professional license. For certified practitioners there are ethical codes of conduct from their certification body. Practitioners who hold a professional license have additional rules, regulations, guidelines, and ethics to follow. In addition, many geographical locations have governmental rules, even laws, covering business and, sometimes, personal behavior. Whether licensed or not, you are responsible for knowing what limitations are placed on your practice, your business, and you as a practitioner in your location.

Representation

Be sure that any advertising, promotions, or professional materials represent an accurate and honest version of your practice and your qualifications. Ensure that any claims regarding past successful outcomes of EFT are based upon full verifiable evidence.

In closing, suffice it to say that the information we have covered in this section on ethics is in no way representative of the full scope of ethical considerations. Please do your own research to determine what is the appropriate code of ethics that applies to you and your business.

Conclusion

This is not the end.

This book is likely one of many you will read on your journey to becoming the best practitioner you can be. If you leave with anything, it should be that the end of this book—the end of any book you read, workshop you attend, certification course you finish—should never actually be the end. There is always more learning to be done. Committing yourself to the ever-evolving field of EFT and energy modalities means committing to a life of continual learning and growth. There is no better way to serve yourself and your clients than to avoid becoming stagnant, to push yourself to continually reach for more, and to continue to develop as a professional. There is so much more information out there, so many more individuals and resources from which you can learn life-changing and practice-enriching information.

We, the authors of this book, are still learning even after our many years of EFT work, and the field itself is evolving every single day. With the closing of this book, we challenge you to continue to challenge yourself. There is no end to what we can accomplish in the world as we move forward together with this groundbreaking modality.

References

AAAAI (American Academy of Allergy, Asthma and Immunology). (2013). Allergy statistics. Retrieved from http://www.aaaai.org/about-the-aaaai/newsroom/allergy-statistics.aspx

Adams, A. (2014, March 27). On being specific [Online article]. Retrieved from http://fromthedeskofannadams.com/on-being-specific

Ader, R., & Cohen. N. (1975). Behaviorally conditioned immunosuppression. *Psychosomatic Medicine, 37*(4), 333–340.

Ader, R., Felten, D. L., & Cohen, N. (Eds.). (2007). *Psychoneuroimmunology* (4th ed., 2 vols.). Boston, MA: Elsevier/Academic Press.

Allen, J. G. (1995). *Coping with trauma: A guide to self-understanding.* Washington, DC: American Psychiatric Press.

Ambady, N., & Rosenthal, R. (1992). Thin slices of expressive behavior as predictors of interpersonal consequences: A meta-analysis. *Psychological Bulletin, 111*(2), 256–274.

American Psychiatric Association. (2103). *Diagnostic and statistical manual of mental disorders* (5th ed.). Washington, DC: American Psychiatric Association.

Archer, S. (2006). More scientific evidence for the mind-body connection. *IDEA Fitness Journal, 3*(1).

Baber, A., & Waymon, L. (2007). *Make your contacts count: Networking know-how for business and career success* (2nd ed.). New York, NY: AMACOM.

Bandler, R., & Grinder, J. (1979). *Frogs into princes: Neuro linguistic programming.* Moab, UT: Real People Press.

Bargh, J., Chen, M., & Burrows, L. (1996). Automaticity of social behavior: Direct effects of trait construct and stereotype activation on action. *Journal of Personality and Social Psychology, 71*(2), 230–244.

Beisser, A. (1971). Paradoxical theory of change. In J. Fagan & I. L. Shepherd (Eds.), *Gestalt therapy now: Theory, techniques, applications.* New York, NY: Harper & Row.

Bennett, M. (2011, December 10). EFT and psychotherapy: Getting all the parts of us working together. Retrieved from http://www.eftfree.net/2011/12/10/getting-all-our-parts-working-together

Bernard, C. (1957). *An introduction to the study of experimental medicine.* New York, NY: Dover Publications.

Bharathan, J. (2009). A creative way to develop EFT setup statements [Online article]. Retrieved from http://www.eftuniverse.com/refinements-to-eft/a-creative-way-to-develop-eft-setup-statements

Blutner, R. (n.d.). Rene Descartes and the legacy of mind/body dualism. Retrieved January 14, 2015, from http://www.blutner.de/philom/mindbody/mindbody.pdf

Bridges, N. A. (2001). Therapist's self-disclosure: Expanding the comfort zone. *Psychotherapy: Theory, Research, Practice, Training, 38*(1), 21–30.

Bruner, P., & Bullough, J. (Eds.). (2009). *EFT and beyond: Cutting edge techniques for personal transformation.* Saffron Walden, UK: Energy Publications.

Cannon, W. (1929). Organization for physiological homeostasis. *Physiological Reviews, 9*(3), 399–431.

Carrington, P. (n.d.). Dr. Patricia Carrington on EFT and depression with discussion of meds [Online article]. Retrieved from http://www.eftuniverse.com/index.php?option=com_content&id=10327&lang=en&view=article

Carrington, P. (2005–2012a). Can there be too many aspects? [Web log post]. Retrieved from http://masteringeft.com/masteringblog/can-there-be-too-many-aspects

Carrington, P. (2005–2012b). Introducing the Choices Method [Web log post]. Retrieved from http://masteringeft.com/masteringblog/introducing-the-choices-methods

Carrington, P. (2005–2014). EFT for schizophrenia [Online article]. Retrieved from http://masteringeft.com/masteringblog/eft-for-schizophrenia-article

Church, D. (2013a). Clinical EFT as an evidence-based practice for the treatment of psychological and physiological conditions. In D. Church & S. Marohn (Eds.), *The clinical EFT handbook: A definitive resource for practitioners, scholars, clinicians, and researchers* (Vol. 1, Introduction, pp. 1–14). Fulton, CA: Energy Psychology Press.

Church, D. (2013b). *The EFT manual* (3rd ed.). Santa Rosa, CA: Energy Psychology Press.

Church, D., & Marohn, S. (Eds.). (2013). *The clinical EFT handbook: A definitive resource for practitioners, scholars, clinicians, and researchers, Vols. 1–2.* Fulton, CA: Energy Psychology Press.

Cohen, I. B. (1957). Foreword. In C. Bernard, *An introduction to the study of experimental medicine.* New York, NY: Dover Publications.

Cohen, S., & Williamson, G. M. (1991). Stress and infectious disease in humans. *Psychological Bulletin, 109*(1), 5–24.

Creswell, J. D., Welch, W. T., Taylor, S. E., Sherman, D. K., Gruenewald, T. L., & Mann, T. (2005). Affirmation of personal values buffers neuroendocrine and psychological stress responses. *Psychological Science, 16*(11), 846–851.

Dane, E., & Pratt, M. G. (2007). Exploring intuition and its role in managerial decision making. *Academy of Management Review, 32*(1), 33–54.

Davidson, K. (2012, June 17). A spin on the apex effect [Online article]. Retrieved from www.howtotap.com/a-spin-on-the-apex-effect

Davidson, K., & Sherrod, K. B. (2013). Aspects. In D. Church & S. Marohn (Eds.), *The clinical EFT handbook: A definitive resource for practitioners, scholars, clinicians, and researchers* (Vol. 1, pp. 209–218). Fulton, CA: Energy Psychology Press.

Dienes, Z., & Berry, D. (1997). Implicit learning: Below the subjective threshold. *Psychonomic Bulletin and Review, 4*(1), 3–23.

Drew, P. (2012). *Creating your elevator pitch: How to communicate value in 20 seconds or less* [Slide program]. United States: Ivyexec.

Ehrnstrom, Colleen. (2011). *Mastering the metaphor.* Presentation given at the ACBS World Conference IX in Boulder, CO.

Elsevier. (2008, August 27). Chronic stress alters our genetic immune response. *ScienceDaily.* Retrieved from http://www.sciencedaily.com/releases/2008/08/080827100816.htm

Engel, G. (1980). The clinical application of the biopsychosocial model. *American Journal of Psychiatry, 137*(5), 101–124.

Feinstein, D. (2010). Rapid treatment of PTSD: Why psychological exposure with acupoint tapping may be effective. *Psychotherapy: Theory, Research, Practice, Training, 47,* 385–402.

Feinstein, D. (2012). Acupoint stimulation in treating psychological disorders: *Evidence of efficacy. Review of General Psychology, 16,* 364–380.

Feinstein, D. (2013). What does energy have to do with energy psychology? In D. Church & S. Marohn (Eds.), *The clinical EFT handbook: A definitive resource for practitioners, scholars, clinicians, and researchers* (Vol. 1, pp. 65–85). Fulton, CA: Energy Psychology Press.

Feinstein, D. (with Eden, D.). (2011). *Ethics handbook for energy healing practitioners.* Fulton, CA: Energy Psychology Press.

Feinstein, D., Eden, D., & Craig, G. (2005). *The promise of energy psychology: Revolutionary tools for dramatic personal change.* New York, NY: Jeremy P. Tarcher/Penguin.

Fernandez, J. V. (1977). The performance of ritual metaphors. In J. D. Sapir & I. C. Crocker (Eds.), *The social use of metaphors: Essays on the anthropology of the rhetoric.* Philadelphia: University of Pennsylvania Press.

Fisher, C. D. (2004). Ethical issues in therapy: Therapist self-disclosure of sexual feelings. *Ethics and Behavior, 12,* 105–121.

Franquemont, S. (1999). *You already know what to do: 10 invitations to the intuitive life.* New York, NY: Jeremy P. Tarcher/Putnam.

Gallo, F. (2000). *Energy diagnostic and treatment methods.* New York, NY: W. W. Norton.

Gallo, F. (2013, March 19). The importance of practitioner self-care, Part 2. Retrieved from http://acepblog.org/2013/03/19/the-importance-of-practitioner-self-care-part-2/

Gallo. F., & Vincenzi. H. (2000). *Energy tapping.* Oakland, CA: New Harbinger Publications.

Garelick, M. G., & Storm, D. R. (2005). The relationship between memory retrieval and memory extinction. *Proceedings of the National Academy of Sciences USA, 102*(26), 9091–9092.

Gazzaniga, M. S. (2012). The storyteller in your head. Discover Magazine, Spring 2012. Retrieved from http://discovermagazine.com/2012/brain/22-interpreter-in-your-head-spins-stories

Giller, E. (1999, May 1). What is psychological trauma? Retrieved from http://www.sidran.org/resources/for-survivors-and-loved-ones/what-is-psychological-trauma

Gruder, D., & Gregory, N. (Ed.). (2006). *Comprehensive Energy Psychology Certification Module: Willingness to Succeed/Psychological Reversals.* Ardmore, PA: Association for Comprehensive Energy Psychology.

Hall, S. (2013, June 17). Neuroscientist Daniela Schiller is researching ways that bad memories can be made less fearsome. *MIT Technology Review.* Retrieved from http://www.technologyreview.com/featuredstory/515981/repairing-bad-memories

Heitler, S. (2012, February 16). Bad luck, bad choices or psychological reversal? *Psychology Today.* Retrieved from http://www.psychologytoday.com/blog/resolution-not-conflict/201202/bad-luck-bad-choices-or-psychological-reversal

Herman J. (2012). Book review of Special issue: Guidelines for treating dissociative identity disorder in adults (3rd rev.); Rebuilding shattered lives: Treating complex PTSD and dissociative disorders; and Understanding and treating dissociative identity disorder: A relational approach. *Psychoanalytic Psychology, 29*(2), 267–269.

Hodgkinson, G. P., Langan-Fox, J., & Sadler-Smith, E. (2008). Intuition: A fundamental bridging construct in the behavioral sciences. *British Journal of Psychology, 99*, 1–27.

Hover-Kramer, D. (2011). *Creating healing relationships: Professional standards for energy therapy practitioners.* Santa Rosa, CA: Energy Psychology Press.

Kaplan, W., Wirtz, V., Mantel-Teeuwisse, A., Duthy, B., & Laing, R. (2013). Depression. *In Priority Medicines for Europe and the World Update Report, 2013* (pp. 135–139). Geneva, Switzerland: World Health Organization.

Karjala, L. (2007). *Understanding trauma and dissociation.* Atlanta, GA: Thomas-Max Publishing.

Kenny, R. (2004). What can science tell us about collective consciousness? [Online article]. Retrieved from http://www.collectivewisdominitiative.org/papers/kenny_science.htm

Launer, J. (2005). Anna O and the "talking cure." *QJM, 98*(6), 465–466.

Look, C. (2010). The importance of testing in EFT [Online article]. Retrieved from www.attractingabundance.com/eft/importance-of-testing

Loue, S. (2008). *The transformative power of metaphor in therapy.* New York, NY: Springer.

McCraty, R., Atkinson, M., & Bradley, R. T. (2004). Electrophysiological evidence of intuition: Part 1. The surprising role of the heart. *Journal of Alternative and Complementary Medicine, 10*(1), 133–143.

Mercola, J. (2012, July 21). Emotional Freedom Technique (EFT) for pain relief [Online article]. Retrieved from http://articles.mercola.com/sites/articles/archive/2012/07/21/eft-for-pain-relief.aspx

Miller, J. P. (2007). *The holistic curriculum.* Toronto, Ontario: University of Toronto Press.

Mitchell, C. W. (2009). *Effective techniques for dealing with highly resistant clients* (2nd ed.). Johnson City, TN: C. W. Mitchell.

Moss, G. (2010, July 10). Emotion and perception: EFT makes it a two-way street [Online article]. Retrieved from http://www.eftfree.net/2010/07/10/emotion-and-perception

Myers, D. G. (2002, November 1). The powers and perils of intuition. *Psychology Today.* Retrieved from http://www.psychologytoday.com/articles/200212/the-powers-and-perils-intuition

National Alliance on Mental Illness (NAMI). (n.d.). What is posttraumatic stress disorder? Retrieved from http://www.nami.org/Template.cfm?Section= posttraumatic_stress_disorder

National Institutes of Health (NIH). (2013). The benefits of slumber: Why you need a good night's sleep. *NIH News in Health,* April 2013. Retrieved from http://newsinhealth.nih.gov/issue/apr2013/feature1

Pert, C. (1999). *Molecules of emotion: Why you feel the way you do.* New York, NY: Scribner.

Pert, C. B., Ruff, M. R, Weber, R. J., & Herkenham, M. (1985). Neuropeptides and their receptors: A psychosomatic network. *Journal of Immunology, 135*(2 Suppl), 820s-826s.

Prince, T. (2010). EFT and the power of reframing [Online article]. Retrieved from http://eftmastersworldwide.com/eft-and-power-of-reframing

Putnam, F. W. (1989). *Diagnosis and treatment of multiple personality disorder.* New York, NY: Guilford Press.

Reber, A. S. (1993). *Implicit learning and tacit knowledge: An essay on the cognitive unconscious.* New York, NY: Oxford University Press.

Roberts, E. (n.d.). Living with cancer and EFT [Online article]. Retrieved from http://www.surrenderworks.com/cancer_and_eft.html

Roberts, E. (2010). *Even though I have cancer.* London, UK: EFT Centre.

Roberts, E. (2013, January 1). Using EFT for trauma. Retrieved from http://www.shiftyourlife.com/2010/a-detailed-and-masterful-article-on-using-eft-for-trauma-by-emma-roberts

Safran, J. D. (2012). *Psychoanalysis and psychoanalytic therapies.* Washington, DC: American Psychological Association.

Sapolsky, R. (2010). This is your brain on metaphors. *New York Times,* November 14, 2011. Retrieved from http://opinionator.blogs.nytimes.com/2010/11/14/this-is-your-brain-on-metaphors

Scaer. R. (2006). Precarious present. *Psychotherapy Networker,* November–December, 49–53, 67.

Schecter, C. (2013). The constricted breathing technique. In D. Church & S. Marohn (Eds.), *The clinical EFT handbook: A definitive resource for practitioners, scholars, clinicians, and researchers* (Vol. 1, pp. 311–313). Fulton, CA: Energy Psychology Press.

Sidran Institute and Enoch Pratt Health System. (1994). What are traumatic memories? Retrieved from http://www.sidran.org/resources/for-survivors-and-loved-ones/what-are-traumatic-memories

Tart, C. (1975). *Transpersonal psychologies.* New York, NY: Harper & Row.

Trafton, A. (2013). Neuroscientists plant false memories in the brain: MIT study also pinpoints where the brain stores memory traces, both false and authentic. *MIT News,* July 25, 2013. Retrieved from http://newsoffice.mit.edu/2013/neuroscientists-plant-false-memories-in-the-brain-0725?Section=posttraumatic_stress_disorder

University of California–Los Angeles (2008, July 16). Mechanism behind mind-body connection discovered. *ScienceDaily,* July 16, 2008. Retrieved from http://www.sciencedaily.com/releases/2008/07/080715152325.htm

Uttl, B., Ohta, N., & Siegenthaler, A. (Eds.). (2006). *Memory and emotion: Interdisciplinary perspectives.* Malden, MA: Blackwell.

Van der Kolk, B. (1994). The body keeps the score: Memory and the evolving psychobiology of posttraumatic stress. *Harvard Review of Psychiatry, 1*(5), 253–265.

Vass, Z. (2012). *A psychological interpretation of drawings and paintings: The SSCA method: Systems analysis approach.* Alexandra Publishing (http://ssca.alexandra.hu).

Vaughan, F. E. (1979). *Awakening intuition.* Garden City, NY: Anchor Press.

Winerman, L. (2005). The mind's mirror. *Monitor on Psychology, 36*(9), 48.

Witztum, E., van der Hart, O., & Friedman, B. (1988). The use of metaphors in psychotherapy. *Journal of Contemporary Psychotherapy, 18*(4), 270–290.

Woldt, A. L., & Toman, S. M. (2005). Gestalt therapy: History, theory, and practice. Thousand Oaks, CA: Sage Publications.

Wolpe, J. (1969). The practice of behavior therapy. New York, NY: Pergamon Press.

Zeidan, F., Martucci, K. T., Kraft, R. A., Gordon, N. S., McHaffie, J. G., & Coghill, R. C. (2011). Brain mechanisms supporting the modulation of pain by mindfulness meditation. *Journal of Neuroscience, 31*(14), 5540–5548.

Zimmerman, E. (2007). Hobbies are rich in psychic rewards. *New York Times,* December 2, 2007.

Appendix A
The EFT Flow Chart
by Ann Adams

When first beginning to use EFT, there can be confusion about when to use which EFT technique. The EFT Flow Chart, developed by Ann Adams, is one of the most popular handouts at her workshops. You can download a copy from http://FromtheDeskofAnnAdams.com

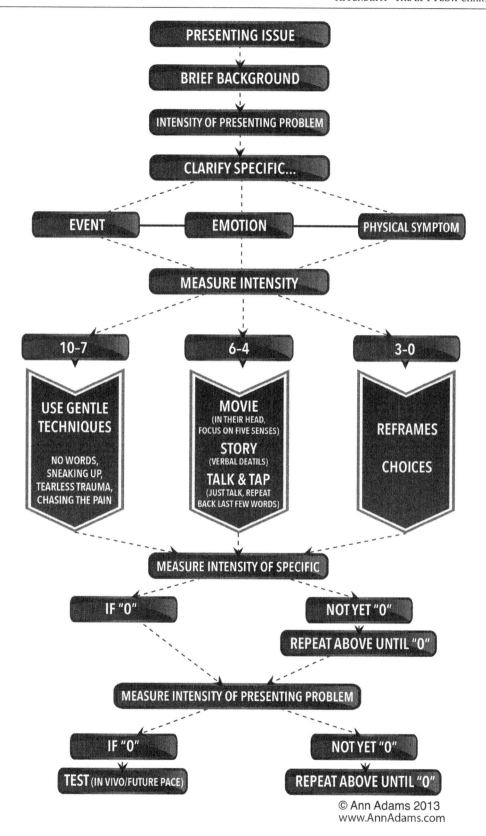

The EFT Flow Chart

Appendix B
Successful Weight Loss with EFT
by Carol Look, LCSW, DCH, EFT Master

[Note by the authors of *EFT Level 3 Comprehensive Training Resource:* It is not possible in any book to cover every potential problem or challenge you or your clients may present. One of the more frequent challenges, however, is the issue of weight loss, an issue with which a large percentage of the population seems to struggle. It is no wonder then that the following article by EFT Master Dr. Carol Look, author of *The Tapping Diet,* is an extremely popular, often downloaded article (see www.CarolLook.com). In order to provide valuable information on this hot-topic issue, Dr. Look has graciously given us permission to share her protocol for EFT and weight loss with you.]

My Successful Weight Loss protocol is divided into four sections: the Present, the Past, the Future, and Extras.

Part 1: The Present

The first section of this article targets the symptom and behavior of emotional overeating, as well as the cravings that accompany it. When clients first contact an EFT practitioner, they often report that these are their "problems": they have terrible cravings and they are unable to control what and how much they eat. Obviously, emotional overeating that temporarily satisfies intense cravings is only a symptom. There are many layers of issues under the symptom of emotional overeating that could be addressed with EFT, but it's often more effective to target these symptoms first, as the client may not be ready to address the underlying emotions or childhood conflicts that trigger them.

When clients see that EFT can help them reduce their cravings, they have hope that they can solve their problems and greater confidence that EFT can help with losing weight permanently. After using EFT to work with cravings, some of the deeper layers of emotional issues have "space" and begin to emerge, and new tapping targets can be addressed with EFT.

There are hundreds of Setup phrases I have used with clients to target their addiction to food and the resulting weight problem. Overeating often feels compulsive to these clients; they are unable to control themselves, a critical feature of addiction.

Setup Statements that address the addictive and compulsive nature of the behavior can be helpful:

Even though I'm a food addict, I deeply and completely accept myself.

Even though I'm obsessed with food, I choose to appreciate who I am.

Even though I can't seem to stop once I start...

Even though I need to eat to feel numb...

Even though I'm a sugar addict and can't stop eating it...

Even though I crave sweets at night...

Even though I have an enormous appetite...

Even though I'm a closet eater and have to satisfy that urge...

Even though I binge at night...

Even though my anxiety makes me need to stuff myself...

Even though I'm eating because of all the stress in my life...

Even though overeating calms me down...

Even though I eat compulsively and can't stop no matter what...

I usually ask the client to tap on themselves three times a day, for 5–10 minutes, using the phrases that accurately address their specific problem. I ask clients to tap in the early morning and in the late evening before they go to bed, as long as they are not in the middle of a struggle to avoid eating at these times. When a client waits to do their tapping until they have a strong craving, they are much less likely to complete the process, although, of course, I invite them to tap during those times as well!

Two Setups that work well to release the cravings of certain clients commonly emerge:

Even though I have an urge to eat whenever I smell food...

Even though I have a craving whenever I see food...

Our sense of smell may trigger cravings, and seeing delicious food is a very powerful anchor—remember, "advertising" works.

Once the cravings are relieved somewhat, the next step is to move on to targeting the underlying emotions, stresses, and anxiety that drive cravings and the behavior of overeating. It has long been known among addiction professionals that addictive behavior is a person's attempt to resolve their underlying anxiety. Food is just another "substance" and overeating another behavior. They are used because they successfully anesthetize or tranquilize strong emotional distress.

Classic phrases that address this connection between emotions and food often hit home with clients:

Even though I eat when I'm bored...

Even though I feel the urge to eat when I'm angry...

Even though I need to eat when I'm lonely...

Even though I overeat to punish myself...

Even though I need to eat to avoid my feelings...

Even though I use food to soothe myself, because I don't know how else to do it...

Even though I overeat to hide myself...

Even though I binge because I think I'm worthless...

Even though I overeat because I don't love myself...

Even though I feel anxious when I can't eat a lot...

Even though I feel so deprived if I can't overeat...

Even though I feel deprived of love so I use food to fill me...

I recommend that you and your clients spend time looking for the phrases that really ring true for them, as this will save a great deal of treatment time in the long run. If the clients call their behavior "stuffing" rather than "overeating," or they report they have strong "desires" instead of "cravings," then make sure to use their words.

In order for clients to enjoy long-term weight-loss success, I find it is essential to focus on two key tapping targets: guilt and self-hatred. Often clients hold on to these emotions, thinking that guilt will push them toward dieting or losing weight or that self-hatred will keep their willpower strong. Unfortunately, these emotions are not motivating factors. In fact, they can make a client eat even more. This "punishment" approach never works, and often backfires. EFT is more effective when practitioners help clients release intense guilt and self-hatred that they feel about overeating, feeling out of control, and being overweight.

Setups that address these self-sabotaging emotions can be very effective:

Even though I hate myself for overeating...

Even though I feel guilty when I overeat...

Even though I feel guilty about being overweight...

Even though I feel ashamed of my body...

Even though I want to hide behind the food and weight...

Tapping on guilt and self-hatred may dramatically reduce anxiety, which, in turn, helps people stay on their food plan and prevent relapse. Remember, overeating works to reduce anxiety, so if we can help our clients reduce their anxiety in a healthier way, they can gain some traction with their weight issues. Sometimes it's helpful to ask clients to tap for forgiveness with such phrases as *"I forgive myself for overeating"* or *"I forgive myself for eating when I'm not hungry"* or *"I forgive myself for overeating when I'm angry."* If they object to saying these phrases, the objection can be excellent feedback for the practitioner. This tells you that, evidently, they need more work on releasing their guilt and shame. All strong emotions need to be addressed with tapping or these clients will inevitably relapse and long-term success will elude them.

A note about guilt: I worked for 8 years at an institute treating alcoholics, addicts, and their family members. The population termed "ACOAs," Adult Children of Alcoholics, deserves special mention. These clients were raised by one or more addicted parents or caregivers. ACOAs often suffer from free-floating guilt that is astoundingly intense. They report feeling a gnawing sense of emptiness and never doing enough that comes from the perception and feeling that they were not a good enough child to make their parent stop drinking. "If only I had been smart enough, good enough, clever enough, etc., Dad would have stopped drinking for me." Of course, this isn't true, but 8-year-olds don't understand addiction! Dig deep with clients who were raised with excessive dysfunction and help them release the irrational guilt that tells them they should have been able to stop the parent from using drugs or alcohol. Without releasing these feelings and reframing this perception, they will not have long-term success with weight loss.

In addition, it's important to note that many ACOAs have sworn off alcohol because of their associations with their addicted parent, yet they haven't addressed the underlying emotional conflicts. They often turn to food as a more "acceptable" substance to neutralize all of their emotions and childhood conflicts. This underlying anxiety from childhood dysfunction and family addiction is often undiagnosed and untreated in children, so that it results in a continuing cycle of drug, alcohol, or food addiction later in life.

Part 2: The Past

In this part of the treatment protocol, I address specific events from a client's childhood. I ask clients to name three of the worst incidents that have hurt their self-esteem and then we tap for the feelings associated with the events. Who hurt them? What did the person say? What embarrassed them or humiliated them? I ask which is the "loudest" memory? The stickiest? The worst? If childhood abuse issues surface, make sure you are equipped to handle this material as a clinician, as the client can be retraumatized if they don't feel safe talking about (and reliving) what happened. In the event that abuse memories surface for the first time for the client (or you), make sure you tread lightly and gently *and seek additional professional help with a practitioner trained in trauma therapy if necessary.*

I also ask clients to picture the first time they discovered food as a "pacifier" and address the underlying emotions that they felt at the time.

Even though I remember turning to food after he yelled at me, I accept who I am and how I feel.

Even though thinking of that memory makes me have cravings right now...

Even though remembering that loneliness makes me want to stuff myself...

Even though I felt so inadequate back then...

Even though I remember her giving me candy when I was upset, and it calmed me down...

I also ask clients about their family's attitude toward food, for instance, what was the emotional atmosphere around the dinner table at home?

This often brings up new emotional material, which I help them form into suitable EFT Setup phrases for their tapping sessions:

Even though I'm anxious whenever I sit down to eat...

Even though I associate food with my parents' fighting...

Even though I associate food with my mother's love...

Even though I feel unsafe without food...

Even though I eat to feel better...

Even though I had to eat to feel safe...

I ask clients to remember the sharpest criticism they've heard regarding their bodies. I ask them to tap for shame or whatever the strongest feelings are that surface when they think of being overweight. This treatment direction can uncover additional upsetting events and time periods that may need more work. Go slowly and respectfully and you will make tremendous headway.

Part 3: The Future

In this phase of treating clients for weight loss, I test them to see how they would feel in the future if they couldn't binge with freedom, or were blocked from satisfying intense cravings, or couldn't use food to shut down their emotions. It is critical for practitioners to address a weight-loss client's future, or it is inevitable that the client will relapse.

I ask clients the following questions and tap for the emotional reaction they give me:

1. "Picture yourself not being able to eat sweets in the evening...How do you feel?" They often respond by saying: "anxious, angry, lonely or irritable." We tap for their response.

2. "Picture yourself as thin as you would like to be. What happens? How do you feel?" This often brings up a variety of answers. Some clients say they

don't deserve to reach their goal weight, or they feel anxious, or they don't feel safe anymore without their "shield" of extra weight. Sometimes they say they don't want other people to be envious of them, or to comment on their body or appearance. We tap for whatever fears and feelings surface.

3. "Picture yourself addressing the underlying feelings that trigger the eating behavior. How do you feel?" They often feel anxious or just "resistant" to exploring their emotions and doing this "homework" and admit that they would rather suffer with the eating and weight problems. Tapping might sound something like this: *"Even though I'm afraid to face my childhood depression..."* or *"Even though I'm afraid to deal with my rage at my father..."* or *"Even though I'm afraid to address the abuse that made me start eating in the first place..."*

Then I address specific sabotaging behaviors and ask clients what their theories are about why they might sabotage weight-loss progress.

I ask them to repeat the following statements out loud and tap for whichever ones cause a reaction:

"It's not safe for me to lose weight."

"It's not safe for others if I lose weight."

"I don't feel supported by my family members..." (I have often heard about clients being offered food to sabotage them just as they are making progress in their weight-loss efforts.)

"I don't deserve to be happy with my body."

I also ask clients to say out loud, "I weigh _____ pounds" (whatever the goal weight is) and see what emotions come up:

Even though I have a block to weighing less than ___ pounds...

Even though I sabotage myself whenever I weigh less than ___ pounds...

Even though I have this comfort zone and can't get below this number...

I also ask them to tap for the following phrases:

Even if I never get over this eating disorder, I accept myself anyway.

Even if I never lose weight, I accept who I am right now.

These two phrases seem to relieve the inevitable feelings of desperation that most people with binge eating habits suffer from on a daily basis. The clients often say they don't want to repeat these phrases because the phrases don't feel "true." I urge them to say the phrases anyway, although you might modify the phrases so that they are more acceptable to the client. You might suggest, for instance, "I'll think about accepting who I am anyway." Saying some statement of acceptance seems to reduce unconscious energetic blocks to losing weight and can help diminish the out-of-control behavior.

Obviously, there are many more phrases and issues you could ask clients to tap for in an EFT session or for "homework" between sessions. It all depends on each client's particular patterns and what might work for that client. The essential emotional targets as far as universal problems with weight loss and cravings seem to be guilt, self-hatred, fear, and anxiety.

Part 4: "Extras"

1. Apparently, restrictive eating, chronic dieting, yo-yo weight gain and loss, and binge eating disturb the balance of the endocrine system and thus metabolism. This is particularly frustrating to clients who think that starving between binges can help them lose weight. The metabolism, expecting to be starved again in the near future, reacts by holding onto every last morsel of food. For some people, this slowing of the metabolism can impede progress in the beginning. This is why you often hear people protest that they don't eat enough food or calories to gain weight, yet they gain anyway! I ask my clients to read up on stress and how it affects the hormonal system, insulin production, and basics of nutrition.

2. I know there is a lot of bad press about low-carbohydrate diets, but talk to a carb or sugar addict or someone who is hypoglycemic, and they will tell you that it *does matter* what kinds of foods they eat and when. They find that breads and sugars trigger a compulsion to eat more breads and sugars. It makes sense when you consider the basic principles of addiction. Alcoholics in AA know that "One drink is too many, and a million isn't enough." This is how a sugar addict feels. Have them tap for *"Even though I'm out of control..."* or *"Even though I'm powerless over food..."* or *"Even though I can't stop once I start..."*

3. Tap for an imbalanced or slow metabolism. People love this target:

    Even though my metabolism is too slow, I choose to regulate it now.

    Even though my metabolism is imbalanced...

4. You can always use daily affirmations such as *"Thank you, Universe, for speeding up my metabolism..."* or *"Thank you, God, for releasing me from compulsive eating..."*

5. I always do the tapping on myself while my clients repeat the exact phrases they want to say. On many occasions, when clients say that they can't repeat, *"I deeply and completely accept myself,"* if I say it out loud first, they eventually follow.

Good luck, and be persistent. Your clients will notice that they begin to "forget" about eating binges and obsessive planning around food. They will begin to engage in activities other than secretive eating or food shopping, hoarding, or bingeing. As the anxiety, fear, and need for protection subside, the need for overeating subsides as well. The weight will begin to come off as the underlying issues are addressed and tapping relieves the basis for the symptomatic behaviors.

About the Authors

Ann Adams

As a licensed clinical social worker with nearly 40 years of experience as a therapist, trainer, supervisor, and administrator, Ann Adams was known as a no-nonsense skeptic about energy medicine. The idea of tapping on points of the body to relieve emotional and physical pain seemed a bit out there—until she was introduced to EFT at a National Association of Social Workers–Georgia Chapter (NASW-GA) conference in 1999. Amazed at the power and potential, she has been an avid convert ever since. Ann Adams is in demand as a presenter and educator for conferences and training programs around the world. With her extensive background, she brings a unique understanding to the challenges other practitioners and helpers face in their clinical and administrative work as well as their personal lives. In the mental health field, Ann supervised dozens of therapists and staffed thousands of client cases. During this time, she conducted many staff training sessions on various mental health topics. Over the years, she has worked closely with the creator of EFT, Gary Craig, on a number of projects, culminating in serving as the director of the former EFT Masters Program. She also received EFT Cert-Honors in Craig's last certification program and holds the ACP-EFT from the ACEP-EFT program. Ann still maintains a small EFT caseload, but now specializes in "helping the helpers." She is a DCEP with the Association for Comprehensive Energy Psychology (ACEP) and was the first American to receive Training of Trainers certification from the Association for the Advancement of Meridian Energy Techniques (AAMET). She has presented EFT topics on Internet radio shows and at many conferences including ACEP, NASW-GA, and the EFT Masterclass in the UK.

Karin Davidson

Karin Davidson, CMT, is an AHP certified international trainer of trainers for EFT, international certified Matrix Reimprinting trainer, certified AMT EFT Master and Trainer, Reiki Master, NGH certified hypnotist, certified in the Emotion Code, and the creator of Prenatal Reimprinting. Karin is cofounder of Alternative and Complementary Healthcare Professionals (www.ACH-Pros.com), the Meridian Tapping Techniques Association, and EFT United, and is honored to be one of Dr. Stephen Adler's faculty members. Karin has also created over 120 training videos in various forms of meridian tapping techniques and energy practices, has presented at events including the EFT Masterclass and EFT Gathering in the UK, and was a featured speaker at the Canadian Association for Integrative and Energy Therapies (CAIET) conference. Karin is trained in Inner Repatterning, Imagineering, EFT for Addictions, Dianetics Auditing, TAT, Z-Point, Arc of Healing, Energy Psychology, Color Healing, the Body Code, and Intuitive Healing. She was one of the team of four who created the certification programs for EFT Universe, Meridian Tapping Techniques Association, and Alternative Healthcare Professionals. Karin also is part of the Israeli Trauma Center Project working with victims of trauma, the Veterans Stress Project, and War on Stress organizations working with veterans. She has been learning and practicing energy medicine tools for over 35 years, and has dedicated her life to teaching others about these revolutionary techniques.

Kari Tumminia

Kari Tumminia is a certified EFT Level 3 practitioner, Matrix Reimprinting practitioner, and Prenatal Reimprinting practitioner. She completed her master's degree at Eastern University in St. David's, Pennsylvania, specializing in research and training in using the creative arts to promote healing, teach skills, and facilitate conflict resolution in at-risk and vulnerable populations. She has worked internationally as a teaching artist for BuildaBridge International, and developed content and curriculum for nonprofits working cross-culturally and with at-risk populations. She has worked with Karin Davidson, filming a long list of EFT and energy modality trainings and conferences, and has applied her research and writing skills to developing a variety of EFT and energy resources, including articles on EFT and the Bible, depression, and others. Kari works with individual clients using energy modalities and the arts, works closely with nonprofits that have dedicated themselves to aiding the most vulnerable members of society, and strives to contribute professional level research and writing to the energy field.

CPSIA information can be obtained
at www.ICGtesting.com
Printed in the USA
LVOW02s0524290916

505468LV00001B/29/P

9 781604 150988